Betty Webb MBE, *Légion d'honneur*, is a one-hundred-year-old veteran who served at Great Britain's secret codebreaking operation at Bletchley Park and the Pentagon in the US during the Second World War. She lives in Worcestershire.

NO MORE SECRETS

BETTY WEBB

My part in codebreaking at Bletchley Park
and the Pentagon

First published in 2023 by Mardle Books
15 Church Road
London, SW13 9HE
www.mardlebooks.com

Text © 2023 Betty Webb

Paperback ISBN 9781837700219
eBook ISBN 9781837700417

Printed in the UK

10 9 8 7 6 5 4 3 2 1

MIX
Paper | Supporting
responsible forestry
FSC® C171272

CONTENTS

CONTENTS

ACKNOWLEDGEMENTS

I would not have been able to write this book without a great deal of encouragement and help. My grateful thanks go to members of my family and to Judith Frames for transcribing the first pages of my handwritten notes. My thanks also go to Kerry Howard for her assurances that 'people really want to know about this' and for helping me with the research, and to Simon Robinson for championing this project. Without him this book would not have seen the light of day.

My thanks also go to Liz Lydekker and Jennifer Galvin for granting me permission to include quotes from letters and memoirs. I am delighted to have my great friends Julia Lydekker and Helen Little with me in the pages of this book. Thank you to the Bletchley Park Trust for inviting me to all their events over the years and providing me with opportunities to tell my story. Also to Dr Thomas Cheetham, Research Officer at the Bletchley Park Trust, and Dean Annison, Museum Archivist at the Trust, for supplying the Motor Transport Corps logbook. And to my editors and publishers at Mardle Books, my thanks for the encouragement to delve deeper into the past and for bringing this book to life.

Also, I give thanks to all the people who have taken the time to talk to me and ask questions. It is through their interest and desire to learn more that I have unleashed more of the memories I have held onto for so long. Finally, I can say there are 'no more secrets'.

AUTHOR'S NOTE

This book started out as a few pages in a notebook, which grew into a slim memoir called *Secret Postings: From Bletchley Park to the Pentagon*. For over a decade, I sold copies of this from the back of the room at the end of each of the two hundred or so talks I have given to promote the story of Bletchley Park.

It was hard for me to share all my memories of my time at Bletchley Park after keeping silent for so long. There was also much I did not know about the Government Code and Cypher School's work, processes and organisation. In this new book, I have rummaged through cupboards and scoured my hoards of papers to delve deeper into the past. I now have a copy of my complete service record from the Ministry of Defence to enable me to pinpoint the dates of my recruitment into the women's branch of the British army during the Second World War, known as the Auxiliary Territorial Service (ATS), as well as the dates I arrived at Bletchley Park and the Pentagon. I have also consulted other sources, such as original records held in the National Archives and various publications, which are listed in the bibliography at the end of this book.

The term codebreaker has become the collective name given to anyone who worked at the Government Code and Cypher School (later known as Government Communications Headquarters [GCHQ]) and its outstations. However, only a small proportion of the staff were actual codebreakers (more accurately, cryptanalysts) and it is important to explain that I wasn't one of them. My part is just that – one of many – combined to form one establishment defeating a common enemy.

A cipher is made by swapping one letter, number or symbol of plain language into another letter or symbol for the purpose of making it unintelligible to anyone without the means to reverse it. A code, meanwhile, substitutes an entire word or phrase with an equivalent word or phrase. They are often used interchangeably to describe the work of Bletchley Park and I use both terms in this way throughout the book. I also refer to codebreakers, rather than cryptanalysts.

This is not a technical book about codebreaking. However, I have included additional information about the German Police Section where I worked during the war, even though I did not know until quite recently that we were dealing with non-Enigma encoded messages coming from the German police. I only learnt of this a few years ago from the author of *The Emperor's Codes*, Michael Smith, and it isn't a subject I have seen appear in many books.

It is a great honour to know I played a small part in breaking the codes that allowed the Allies to comprehend the atrocities committed during the Holocaust. Most of the truly horrific reports were sent by the Enigma machine and were dealt with by the codebreakers in Hut 6, but the non-machine traffic, which was composed with pencil and paper, was important because it revealed some of the ruthlessness on the Russian front. These hand-cipher messages also offered a way into the Enigma keys through repetition, when the Germans sent the same information by hand cipher and the Enigma machine.

AUTHOR'S NOTE

For those who enjoy the technical history of codebreaking, I have also included in Appendix 1 a transcription of the official history of the German Police Section, which was written immediately after the war for inclusion in the GCHQ's collection of section histories, now held at the National Archives in Kew (HW3/155). There is also a select glossary of terms at the end of the book.

I do not cover the Japanese Military Section in as much detail, because it is covered with more skill elsewhere, in *The Emperor's Codes* in particular, which was the first publication to mention my name and which was the spark that led to so many opportunities I have since had to talk about my time at Bletchley Park.

The research undertaken for this book has uncovered new information about my time there; it feels strange to reach my one hundredth birthday and still be learning about myself.

CHAPTER 1

CIVILIAN TO SERVICE

Thinking back, I can see myself as an eighteen-year-old listening to the news on the wireless, wishing I could do more for the war effort. That May afternoon was the start of a journey that would take me from the Government Code and Cypher School's covert operation at Bletchley Park, during the war in Europe, to the Pentagon in Washington D.C. until the end of the war against Japan.

It was May 1941 and I was halfway through a domestic science course at Radbrook College near Shrewsbury, learning how to cook, run a house and do household accounts. I was on the course because my parents thought it was a good idea, but I was less enthusiastic. I spent much of my two terms there in the infirmary with the measles and chickenpox, reading *Gone with the Wind* by Margaret Mitchell as a refuge against the boredom. Illness exacerbated my dissatisfaction and the time I spent in class cooking colourless food with limited rations did little to improve my mood. It was hard to focus when bombs dropped during the Blitz lay waste to over one million homes and killed an estimated forty-three thousand people between September 1940 and May 1941. Listening to more bad news over the wireless, I longed to do more for the war effort, especially as I turned eighteen on 13 May that year and I was required to sign up for war work under the Essential Work (General Provisions) Order of March 1941. Four of us left Radbrook shortly afterwards to join up.

Enlisting in the women's armed forces was voluntary until conscription for women between the ages of twenty and thirty came into force in December 1941. I could choose between the ATS, the Women's Royal Naval Service (WRNS, officially and unofficially known as the Wrens) or the Women's Auxiliary Air Force (WAAF). I had seen posters on advertising boards and in newspapers, but had little understanding of the function each service provided. Two of the girls from Radbrook joined the WAAF but I decided to apply for the WRNS based on the qualifications I had gained through home schooling and, like many other women, the attractiveness of the service uniform. It was dark blue, designed by a fashion designer and came with a stylish hat. One of the other girls, Deborah Anne Kennett, also applied to the WRNS. She was born in 1924 in Port Said, Egypt. Her father died of pneumonia in 1932 while working for the Administrative Colonial Service Nigeria and her mother had a wonderful-sounding job as an artist for an archaeological faculty at Cambridge University. She was also a senior warden of the Air Raid Precautions (ARP) from 1939, so would have been supportive of Deborah's plans to enlist. Deborah was accepted for the WRNS, but I was told there was a halt to recruitment there, so I applied to the ATS. No matter the route we took, Deborah and I both ended up at Bletchley Park and became friends.

Established by Royal Warrant on 9 September 1938, the ATS became 'an organisation whereby certain non-combatant duties in connection with Our Military and Air Forces may from time to time be performed by women'. The Secretary of State for War announced that the ATS would receive full military status to encourage more women to enlist. On 25 April 1941, The Defence (Women's Forces) Regulations 1941 brought together all women employed in medical, dental, nursing and auxiliary branches of the army and air force as 'members of the armed forces of the Crown'. Two months later, on 1 July 1941, these services gained the same military status as the men's army, which meant they were no longer considered volunteer services.

By the time I joined on 3 September 1941, the ATS had grown from 17,000 to 65,000 recruits in the United Kingdom. Its military status ensured that female officers received a rank and commission in the same way as their male counterparts, but we did not get equal pay.

As more men joined the war, more women volunteered for national service. The continued pressure to support the war effort prompted the National Service Act (No. 2) in December 1941, which made all unmarried women between the ages of twenty and thirty years old, subject to exceptions, liable for service in one of the women's auxiliary services. Many others worked in factories, where the pay was better, manufacturing essential items for the war effort.

By September 1943, the number of women serving in the ATS peaked at 212,500 and then declined gradually to 190,800 by June 1945. Overall, some 290,000 women served in the ATS during the war, compared to about 74,000 WRNS. The ATS was disbanded in 1949 and replaced by the Women's Royal Army Corps (WRAC).

CHAPTER 2

LIFE IN THE COUNTRYSIDE

Life in the ATS came as a culture shock after growing up in Richard's Castle, a village of half-timbered black and white houses nestled in the scenic countryside on the border of Herefordshire and Shropshire. My childhood home, Ryecroft, is still tucked away in three acres of grassland along Woodhouse Lane on the Herefordshire side of Richard's Castle. I enjoyed an idyllic childhood surrounded by nature, with nothing but the sound of the birds and the breeze in the trees. It was a million miles away from living in close quarters with hundreds of other girls at the ATS training camp, where space and privacy were rare.

I had no experience of sharing a classroom with other children to prepare me for the ATS because my parents had preferred home schooling. My mother, Charlotte Cecelia (nee Harris), spent part of her day giving us lessons, while my father, Leslie Thomas Vine-Stevens, worked as a bank clerk for Lloyds Bank. He rode the four and a half miles to the bank in Ludlow on a motorbike or trudged there on foot in deep snow.

However, before Ryecroft, we lived in the small village of Aston on Clun located twelve miles north of Ludlow in a house called The Villa, where I was born on 13 May 1923. I was named Charlotte, after my mother, but everyone knows me as Betty. My brother David followed on 31 January 1925.

We must have moved to Richard's Castle soon after David was born, because my clearest childhood memory of the village is connected to his illness. I was four and David was two and he had struggled with ill health since his birth, but this time was different. My parents sent me to stay with the Hall family, who lived on the southern edge of the village and were always happy to offer a helping hand when needed. People in a small community understood the necessity of looking out for one another, even when they had little to spare themselves.

I am not sure how long I stayed away; I only remember walking home with Betty, the Hall's daughter. On seeing Granny at the door, I asked, 'Where is David?' and Granny told me to 'shush'. I don't recall ever being told David had died, but I must have understood this even in my limited understanding and by his permanent absence from that day onwards. The memory of Granny's strained 'shush' is still vivid; perhaps she thought I would add further distress to my parents' grief. They shouldered the burden quietly and never discussed David's death with me, not even as I grew older. In fact, I only discovered he had died on a Friday, the 14 September 1927, from meningitis, in the course of writing this book.

It must seem strange that it has taken me over ninety-five years to learn the reason for my brother's death, but back then, it was the way of things. You did as you were told, didn't ask questions and just got on with things as best you could. As I reflect on those years, I am sure the stoicism I learnt from a young age provided the foundation for who I am today. Had I not been so obedient, I would not have accepted with such readiness the opportunities awaiting my eighteen-year-old self as she buttoned up her ATS uniform for the first time.

David's death certificate refers to our home as The Bungalow, but I only know it as Ryecroft. It had an extensive view, from Clee Hill (Titterstone) in the east along to Abberley and Stoke Edith, and I have lived nowhere else with a view to compare. I often say now that I have a nice outlook into my garden, but I don't have a view.

From 1943, a shortwave radio transmitting station was built in the nearby village of Woofferton, with a grid of masts sticking out of the ground like pins holding down the patchwork of the countryside. They annoyed me and I complained at every opportunity that they ruined the view from the house. Yet, I felt the opposite when looking up towards the house from the road in Woofferton. When the mist didn't hang on the hill, I felt a tug as Ryecroft came into view from the road. Many trees – copper beech, Spanish and horse chestnut, Norwegian spruce, yew – and many varieties of flowers and shrubs surrounded the house. The branches of the chestnut by the hedge were perfect for dangling upside down, with the back of my knees bearing the scratches of my fun.

The land was sectioned into garden and produce. The vegetable beds overflowed and there was an orchard of pear, plum and apples trees, a small apiary for beehives, a barn for goats and pigs, and poultry surrounded by lawns and meadows. Messrs Stephens, the local grocer in Ludlow, travelled round the village in his van collecting orders one week and delivered them to the house the following week, so we could get anything we needed to supplement our home-grown supplies.

There was no gas, electricity nor mains water, so heating was by open coal or wood fires and we pumped water from a well beneath the bungalow. We cooked and baked bread with Valor paraffin stoves and lit the house with paraffin lamps and candles.

The latrines at Ryecroft were a scramble across the grass from the house, which was not funny when it was pouring with rain or one was ankle deep in snow. The journey started at the back door, then along the hedge adjacent to the house, past the back of the beehives to the honeysuckle-covered privy. A towering yew tree cloaked its existence from those not knowing where to look. It was amusing to watch guests trying to find their way to it, in haste and in the dark, without disturbing the bees.

What we lacked in 'mod cons' was more than compensated for in the lush countryside, the fresh air and freedom of the open space. I remember I slept in a tent in the garden for most of the summer with no worries about thieves or traffic, and with only the wildlife as company. On fine nights, I pulled my makeshift bed out of the tent and slept in the open air so that I could lie and gaze at the stars and into the infinite depths of the sky. Although the long days and fair weather of summer were a child's delight, they were also a smallholder's headache when the well, the underground water tank and the water butts dried up and the earth baked so hard the water evaporated before it penetrated the vegetable roots. We were always frugal with water, regardless of the weather. My mother considered one bowl of clean water enough to wash the vegetables, then the dishes, and anything remaining was poured over plants in the garden. The rainwater we collected in water butts was the primary source of water for the plants, so we collected as much as possible. There was no such thing as a daily shower in those days, just a flannel and a bowl on the washstand to wipe away the worst of the grime and a weekly bath in front of the fire. Any bathing at all was out of the question during long droughts.

Other extremes of weather were no less of a problem. There seemed to be more snow in those days, and it lodged in the corrugated iron roof gables and seeped into the bedrooms and froze on the inside of the glass. My father had a telephone installed in the early 1930s, which came in handy when the snowdrifts were so deep we had to call a neighbour to ask them to help dig us out. One winter after the war, the drifts were as high as the hedges. Once the weather warmed, the snow would turn to slush, then melt into floods of water to be churned into muddy pools by the animals.

My sister, Kathleen, known by her middle name Margaret, arrived in the bedroom next to mine during the night of 29 September 1930. The following year, Mother had a mastectomy followed by radium treatment in Birmingham. She was one of the first to receive treatment that combined surgery with radium therapy, which removed the cancer to everyone's relief. The treatment was not as advanced as it is today and survival rates were low, especially with the high risk of sepsis. Mother battled with intense post-operative pain for the rest of her life and her health was a constant worry to us all.

Mother must have had an iron will, for she carried on with so much for another thirty years before she died: coping with the animals, teaching us and doing endless charitable things in the village. We were fortunate, because Mother also had the help of Tante Moderau in the 1930s and later Clara Mandli (later Buchmann) from

Zurich. I believe the Moravian Church, which my mother was connected to, had a hand in these arrangements. Nonetheless, Margaret and I had to help with the chores from a young age, collecting water, wood and eggs and feeding the animals.

There was a lot of unemployment and poverty during the early 1930s and there were always lads and lassies available to do jobs in the house and garden, who were paid for their work with a meal. We also had an abundance of home-grown produce to trade for their skills. My mother also helped some of the unemployed men in the village learn new skills and arranged for a man from Hereford to give classes in basket weaving. We grew osiers, a type of willow, which was used to make the baskets.

My mother could make a busy person look idle, yet she made the most of snatched moments of leisure time. She was a church organist, an accomplished pianist and sang at one time in a choir conducted by Sir Edward Elgar. She would help us go to sleep every evening by playing classical music and also taught us how to play.

My father worked hard at the bank, disappearing from home on his motorcycle each morning and coming home by supper in the evening. On his time off, he tinkered with the motorcycle in the garage at the end of the drive close to the road. He also worked hard in the garden, mowing the lawns and weeding the vegetable beds.

During the early 1930s, he came into some money and used it to renovate our home. For the duration of the work, we moved to Court House, an early seventeenth-century house of two halves. One half was black timbered with white walls and a second floor jutting out over the first floor like it had been stacked on top. The other half resembled a stone cottage. Inside, it had a large fireplace with the original dark wood panelling lining the walls. This may have inspired my father to install panelling, albeit using a lighter wood, in our renovated bungalow.

A few metres west of Court House sat a seventeenth-century circular dovecote with a conical roof and nineteen tiers housing six hundred bird boxes. It is empty now, but during our time in the house some birds still nested there. I found watching the birds much more interesting than following Mother across the road to the village hall to endure another Women's Institute (WI) meeting presided over by a Mrs Salwey, although the cake or a teaspoon of jam helped to alleviate the boredom. I felt much the same about my father's favourite hobby: cricket. At least the WI meetings didn't go on all day.

My father played for the Ludlow and South Shropshire team, which played at a cricket ground eight miles away from home. Mother often made afternoon tea for the players with home-made bread and cake, which she loaded into the basket of her bicycle and rode all the way to the ground in time for the men to leave the pitch.

We returned to our newly modernised, larger, brick bungalow situated in an elevated position, the large porch windows rested high in the walls to take full advantage of the views over the countryside. My bedroom looked out over Abberley and, when I returned during the war, that view seemed like new to me. I found that if I did not drop my gaze too much, I could almost ignore the transmitter station masts.

My parents held the occasional luncheon party at home and Mother would boast that everything on the table was home produced. Our self-sufficiency was the only time she displayed any noticeable self-satisfaction about our lives. And who can blame her; it was all-consuming work. At one such lunch, I dampened her glory by asking whether a chicken she had served up was Hilda. My poor mother. What an awful thing to say. No doubt my parents put me in my place, but I don't recall it. At least we did not have guests for dinner on the day we found one of our goats on the dining table. I suppose we could have joked that we had very fresh milk.

Holt's bus ran a route into Ludlow twice on Saturdays and once on a Monday, stopping at every house if needed. It was always full of chattering cottagers and smallholders taking baskets of produce to the Ludlow Market. The cottagers waited until they saw the bus approach along the lane before leaving their cottages, forcing the bus to slide to a stop when they appeared in the road without warning. There would be cries of 'Oh my God, my eggs' in a broad Herefordshire accent from anyone who did not have a sufficient grip on their basket. Those with larger quantities to sell took their produce by pony and trap. Cars were still rare in the countryside in those days.

Before we got a family car in 1938, we caught a lift to the train station with Jack Pugh, a local farmer, who would take us by pony and trap. It is a slow way to travel the three miles, especially when one is exposed to the elements. I can still remember the intense cold and feel the stinging chilblains in winter. We jumped off at Woofferton Station, a busy junction back then on the Great Western Railway lines to Birmingham and the North–South line between Crewe and Bristol. It was our gateway to the outside world, which at that time, was mostly Granny's house in Weston-Super-Mare.

Many of my later adventures started and finished at this train station. I would get off the train and telephone home, then wait at the Salwey Arms across the road until my father arrived to pick me up. The train station no longer exists, but the pub is still open.

I spent most of my childhood with my family and never had a crowd of girls of my age to play with. My parents taught us to occupy ourselves and keep busy, a lesson that has stood me well all this time. Life was very quiet, so we were used to a slower pace of life. I never minded being alone, but I made friends with the daughter of a local farmer. She had a heart condition, so her parents would not allow her to go to school or do anything energetic. She died aged just seventeen.

In the new village church, All Saints, there was a strict hierarchy to the seat order at services. The Salweys sat in the front row of the left-hand aisle. Behind them sat Captain Ronnie Wallace and the Kennedy family from the Lodge, and the Windsor-Clives (Clive of India). We sat behind them. On the right-hand side, the Betton-Fosters and the Alcock family had pride of place and the rest of the community gathered behind them.

Mrs Alcock played the organ for the services. She was Leipzig conservatoire-trained and was an excellent musician. Mother played the organ from time to time, putting her music talent to good use. Both had to wrestle with the organ, which required water from the local well, called Boney Well, to activate the bellows. The water supply was sometimes unreliable, because it also supplied water to some houses between the well and the church. When the water level was low, we would jokingly say, 'Oh no, the lord of the manor must be running a bath again.'

The village dedicated the church clock in memory of the fourteen men who died in the First World War and their names were engraved on a large tablet mounted on a wall inside the church. After the Second World War, the parish added a smaller plaque in the shape of a ribbon below the tablet to commemorate the only soldier from the village to perish between 1939 and 1945. Private John Reginald Haggart of the Royal Army Medical Corps 16th Parachute Field Ambulance died in action on 17 September 1944 in Arnhem and was buried in the Arnhem Oosterbeek War Cemetery, Netherlands. There is also a Roll of Honour beside the tablet celebrating those who served during the war and I am proud to say my name is included there.

I call the All Saints Church the 'new' church because Richard's Castle has another older church on the south side of the village, which dates back to the twelfth century. The church of St Bartholomew is a half-mile walk along the same track as Court House. It has a separate bell tower dating from the fourteenth century and the ruins of the castle date back to the Domesday Survey (1086) when Osbern Fitz Richard owned the land. Hence the village's name: Richard's Castle.

The Salwey family had been the lords of the manor for hundreds of years, since Colonel Richard Salwey, secretary to Oliver Cromwell, built a house in the mid-1600s on land nestled between Richard's Castle and Ludlow. Another member of the family had Moor Park house built on the same estate a hundred years later, and many of the farms and houses around Richard's Castle fell within the boundary of the estate. The Salweys continued to be central figures in the village and Moor Park remained a defining feature long after the Salweys sold the house in the late 1800s. Lancing College evacuated its students from Sussex to Moor Park during the Second World War and reconfigured it to accommodate the school, which has suited the subsequent schools inhabiting the estate to this day.

As a community we trundled along, following the same traditions as the generations before us, removed from the noise and glare of the wider world. We tended our land and shared the burden of a hard rural existence. It's impossible to remember those bucolic years without a touch of nostalgia, especially in contrast to what was to come. It remains 'home', even though I lived there for such a small proportion of my long life.

Chapter 3

EDUCATION

My parents educated Margaret and me under the Parents' National Educational Union (PNEU) system, which is based on the methods of Charlotte Mason, who believed in educating the whole child. The system provided a structured curriculum for teachers and parents with home-schooled children that focussed on a broad spectrum of subjects taught in a practical way, rather than in a rigid school situation and learning by rote. As well as reading, writing and mathematics, we learnt about music through listening and playing, and learnt about nature by spending a lot of time in the countryside, observing the wildlife and sketching leaves and flowers as part of the syllabus. I still have my sister's exercise books filled with coloured drawings and annotations in ink. Studying nature in this way was the catalyst for my lifelong love of birds and gardening.

In 1935, we travelled by train to a conference for parents and children following the PNEU system held at its headquarters in Ambleside, in the Lake District. I was twelve and recall dressing up for a pageant as Lady Elizabeth Woodville, the tragic wife of King Edward IV and mother of the two princes locked away in the Tower of London, because she had lived for a time in Ludlow.

I also remember meeting Pleione and Martha Kingdon Ward, the daughters of Francis Kingdon Ward, the botanist and explorer whose name I saw in a memorial garden in Canada many years later. We became friends and kept in touch for several years. On one occasion at the conference, I came across them squabbling, so I took their hands and said words to the effect of, 'Come on, girls. Stop that.' The fight broke up and I went on my way thinking no more about it, but someone had seen me and was impressed with my handling of the situation, especially as the girls were only a few years my junior. When I turned eighteen, someone from the PNEU contacted my parents to ask if I might be interested in training as a teacher at the Ambleside headquarters, but I didn't think I had sufficient knowledge to teach.

My untraditional education affected my confidence in some areas for most of my life. Even now, I consider I am well-educated, but not sufficiently qualified. I had plenty of drive to work and built up job experience to compensate, but back then, I had none of the certificates expected for a teacher. In the end, I declined the offer to teach because I had enlisted in the ATS and was waiting for my call-up papers. Would I have entered teaching had I not joined up? Perhaps, but only as an alternative to the dreaded domestic science college.

Mother was a dedicated teacher and shared her love of music with us during every piano and singing lesson. We also learnt to play the violin, but had a different teacher for those lessons. I found the violin a very difficult instrument to learn, despite an initial interest. Mother patiently listened to my screeching practices on the violin and tolerated my lack of dedication on the piano. I am sure I could have been a better pianist if I had worked harder, but if nothing else I learnt to appreciate music, and classical music is still an important part of my life.

In readiness for exams in the late 1930s, I began private tuition with Miss Lucy Winifred Faraday (a relative of Michael Faraday, the scientist) at her home in the neighbouring village of Orleton. One might assume that behind the wooden door, I would find a provincial private tutor, but Miss Faraday was so much more. Born in 1872, she applied for and won a scholarship to study at Owens College, a part of Victoria University in Manchester. The university first admitted women to the college in 1883, subject to stringent restrictions. Such things did not deter Miss Faraday and she graduated with a first class Bachelor of Arts in English Language and Literature. Over the next few years, Miss Faraday became a university fellow, gained a Master's degree, became the first woman elected to the Manchester Literary and Philosophical Society and completed a teaching diploma. Women teachers at the time had to choose between having a career or marriage, as they were required to resign on marriage and focus on what was considered to be the primary concern of a woman, the family.

Whether Miss Faraday taught out of passion or necessity, she must have witnessed many changes in the education of girls between 1903 and the Second World War. She moved to Orleton after retiring from teaching and shared the house with her two sisters. Ethel Richmond Faraday was the eldest and graduated from Owens in 1895, becoming a published author, a playwright and a private tutor who co-authored a book with Lucy in 1933. The youngest sister of the three by a decade, Alice, was an artist and architect's draughtswoman.

My memory is that Mother arranged my mathematics tuition with Miss Faraday because, as she said, 'I hardly knew ninety-nine was nearly a hundred!' Since learning

Miss Faraday's degree was in English literature, I am not so sure. Regardless of the subject, I am quite clear I found Miss Faraday frightening. Not that she was strict, but there was something about this formidable woman I found intimidating as a young girl. Even with her help, nothing could change the fact that I was *hopeless* at exams and never achieved a good result. I was better with languages and picked up German during my youth, taught myself Spanish and took Norwegian lessons later in life.

I had a bicycle then, borrowed from some friends. I used a piece of wood for the seat, so it was terribly uncomfortable. It wasn't a patch on my first bicycle, which had been brand new and bought for me by friends of my parents. Mother was horrified to find they had paid five pounds for it. I must have outgrown it and passed it on to my sister because we threw nothing away.

Tired from my lessons with Miss Faraday, I had to cycle home, which involved a steep hill I named 'Pig Hill' because it was a pig to cycle up. The bicycle was a heavy beast to push up the hill, which became steeper the further I had to push. If I was not careful, it was easy to topple over. I remember falling off into a patch of nettles on one ride home and riding home with stinging skin. The bicycle also had no gears, so I would build up as much speed as I could before reaching the hill and pedal hard to get as far as possible before dismounting and pushing it the rest of the way to the top. Sometimes a pony and trap would come the other way before I had made much progress. Then I would have to dismount and move to the verge while it trundled past, as the roads were just wide enough for a cart. At the crest of the hill, the road dropped away and it was a downhill dash for most of the way home.

CHAPTER 4

TRAVELS IN HITLER'S GERMANY

It has always surprised me that nobody tried to stop Mother travelling to Germany to work as a music teacher on the day Great Britain declared war on Germany on 4 August 1914. After all, tensions had been near boiling point since Bosnian Serb Gavrilo Princip assassinated the Austrian Archduke Franz Ferdinand and his wife, Sophie, on 28 June the same year.

As soon as Mother stepped across the border into Germany, the customs officials detained her temporarily, telling her that as she was now classed as the enemy, she was obliged to report to the local police station each day. There was no way to hop back on the train and go home – it would take time to arrange a safe passage home – so she made her way to the school in Leipzig, where she discovered that Great Britain and Germany were at war. Mother then had to arrange for an emergency passport at the United States Embassy in Berlin, but while she waiting she continued to teach at the school and reported daily to the police station as instructed, where she became on friendly terms with the staff. Her emergency passport eventually arrived on 15 July 1915, granting her permission to travel under the protection of the American Embassy. It was stamped in red on the top right-hand corner with the words: 'Good during the war between

England and Germany', followed by another stamp excluding her from travelling in the 'zone of the armies'. She could now travel safely home to my grandmother in Weston-Super-Mare via Brussels on a three-day permit, arriving in Tilbury, a port town in Essex, on 8 August.

I never had the opportunity to talk more about my mother's time in Germany and now I have a lot of questions. I know that part of the reason she chose to travel to Germany at that time was her connection with the Moravian Church. However, her limited understanding of German complicated her life there and so she set about learning the language and grew to love it. She was determined when we came along that my sister and I would learn the language. However, it is one thing to speak a language, but quite another to understand its dialects and colloquialisms.

My first experience of Germany came in 1937 through an exchange visit with Elisabeth Paul (pronounced Powell), a Moravian who lived in Herrnhut in the Görlitz District of Saxony – the birthplace of the Moravian Church. She came to stay with us for three months to improve her English and, in return, I spent three months at her home improving my German. Elisabeth and I were of a similar age, but had very different personalities and dissimilar backgrounds. She was short and wore round spectacles, with her blonde hair in two long plaits. We went for long walks in the countryside after lessons and on various trips to places nearby.

As July turned to August 1937, we set off from the Ludlow train station for Germany, stopping off first in London, where my great uncle Cecil gave us a whistle-stop tour of the city to fill the hours until our next train to Harwich. We had to haul our luggage around with us and had quite a bit of it as it was customary at the time for the washing to be done every six weeks.

We boarded a ferry from Harwich to Flushing in the Netherlands, where we then boarded a train to Germany. It was my first trip aboard, but I wasn't nervous. I had grown up travelling by train without adult supervision. Back then, it was acceptable to send a child on the train unaccompanied and expect the train guards to keep an eye on them until someone met them from the train at the end of the journey.

I did not see a Nazi uniform during my time in Germany, but I experienced plenty of civilians saying Heil Hitler and slicing the air with their Hitler salute. My impression was of a sense of discomfort and a requirement to follow orders, rather than a zeal for the regime. In retrospect, it was a strange experience and I wish I could remember more details about it.

The last leg of the overnight train journey to Dresden was very tiring and uncomfortable. I found it impossible to sleep and felt miserable. I was terribly homesick throughout the journey, which is about a thousand miles due east of Ludlow. After four days of travel, it was a relief to arrive in Dresden, where Elisabeth's mother and Tante Moderau met us and showed us something of the city before travelling to the Paul family home in Herrnhut.

The family lived in a first-floor apartment with a balcony overlooking the countryside, which seemed so tiny and enclosed compared to the sprawling wildness of home. Elisabeth introduced me to her father, Gerhard Paul, and Erdmuth, her sister. I soon settled down and began to enjoy my visit. My German was reasonable and improved during my stay, although it was not good enough to do essays or exams.

Herrnhut was home to the main Brüdergemeine (Moravian Church). It was a quiet and understated community, centred on the church. Men and women sat separately, on opposite sides of church, during services and the women wore white bonnets made of pretty netting and tied under the chin with ribbons of different colours. Widows wore a bonnet with black ribbons, married women had blue ribbons and single women wore pink ribbons, which must have been the colour of the ribbons I wore during my stay.

The clothing styles were similar to those in England. I remember sleeping under a sort of duvet, similar to what we commonly use today. It seemed strange to me at the time, because we were still using sheets and blankets at home. It was common in German houses to have a solid fuel *ofen* – an enclosed stove in the centre of the room for heat and cooking. There was a shortage of butter during my visit. I know not why! The family loved music and played together at home, and it was fun for me to join in. Sometimes the choir in church was accompanied by four string instruments and listening to the violin inspired me to learn to play when I returned home.

During my stay in Herrnhut, I was included in many social events, including family weddings and christenings. I still have a small green photograph album with photographs of a trip to an outdoor swimming spot in Kunnersdorf, a town within the district, which had a high diving platform. I have a photograph of everyone queuing for a turn to jump in the water but I only watched from the picnic blanket.

I also attended school, which started at 7 am and ended at 1.30 pm. The afternoons were always filled with sports. There is a photograph of me wearing a sleeveless white

22

blouse and skirt covered by a white embroidered full apron. I am holding a book and a long cone of some sort in my arm, and I have a big smile across my face. On the rear of the photograph there is a caption in German 'on the first day of school you get a candy bag'. One particular day that stands out in my mind is the day I went with the school to a farm on the Czech border to harvest potatoes; I was stiff the next day.

In school, we were obliged to stand to attention and give the Hitler salute at the beginning and end of every class. I was fourteen and did not fully grasp the German threat, but felt it was diplomatic to join in with the class requirement to salute. The previous year, the English football team had been pressured by the football association into giving the Nazi salute before an international game in Germany. The player who refused was dropped by the team. I disguised my discomfort at taking part in the class salute by waving my arms, but not joining the verbal salute. I certainly felt an undercurrent of concern.

Elisabeth and Erdmuth belonged to the girls' wing of the Hitler Youth, which had been a legal requirement since the end of 1936 for ethnic Germans and German citizens who were free of hereditary diseases. The Hitler Youth had become the only legally permitted youth group for girls soon after Hitler came to power in 1933 as a way to indoctrinate young girls and boys into Nazi ideals and to train the girls to become good wives and mothers. At fourteen, Elisabeth would have been in the Bund Deutscher Mädel (League of German Girls) and Erdmuth, at twelve, part of the Jungmädelbund (Young Girls' League), although I was not aware of the difference at the time. They disappeared every Sunday morning, but I was not allowed to attend as a guest.

Herr Paul did try to convey to me the local anxiety about the political situation and the Hitler regime, but my German was not good enough to fully comprehend his words. I was aware that Herr and Frau Paul were unhappy that their children had joined the Hitler Youth movement, but it was never openly discussed by the parents and Elisabeth never talked to me of it.

I remember an anxious time when Erdmuth was very ill with scarlet fever and, even though we all shared wooden bunks in the same room, I was lucky enough not to catch it. Living with the family and meeting their friends and relations was a good experience, but I was glad to go home. The journey home was no less tiring and without Elisabeth for company. I kept in touch with the Paul family until war broke out and I lost contact, which I regret. I still have a postcard Herr Paul sent to my parents and it brings back many fond memories of my time with his family:

Dear Mr. Vine-Stevens
Herewith I thank you for the friendly-sent views of Betty. Furthermore I confirm to you the receipt of the 50 Deutschmarks which I received in two traveller cheques from your bank, which I handed over to your daughter Betty. Betty is very happy with my 2 girls, especially Elisabeth, we see them often happy together. We, my wife and I, have become quite fond of Betty, as she integrates with our family and also helps my wife in the household. In school it seems that she understands almost everything well, her German speaking becomes better every day! We often play music together, which we all love a lot! We already look for a companion for the return journey for Betty. I myself have a lot of work to do with the creation of my business premises.

With best regards to you and your wife,
I am very sincerely
Gerhard Paul

After the war, Herrnhut was allocated to the Soviet occupation zone. Years later, Elisabeth or her sister sent me a publication in the post, but I can't recall what it was about. I did not feel able to reply in case it started a series of correspondence, with the potential for unwanted questions about the war. Also, there was the issue of censorship regarding writing to East Germany. I did not want to do anything that might raise concern that I was not honouring my oath of secrecy sworn at Bletchley. Now, I wonder what became of the family.

In the summer of 1938, we went on a rare family holiday to Fairbourne on the Welsh coast. There I met my first 'boyfriend', Otto Stoetzer. I was fifteen and he was seventeen. He was on holiday from Hamburg, Germany, and was fluent in German, Spanish and French; I thought he was the 'bee's knees' and was delighted to be able to air my German. I have a photograph of us together beneath a tree with his arm around my waist. I am looking very pleased with myself, but a lasting romance was not to be.

We corresponded until war broke out and met again after the war, neither of us discussing our part in the conflict. Later, he was the author of a number of books and regularly sent me the Spanish version of the Organisation of American States magazine from Buenos Aires following his move there, so I was able to keep up my limited Spanish and learn a lot about South America.

In 1938, seventeen-year-old Dorothea Schiffer joined us from Breslau in Germany. Her father was Jewish and a medical doctor. Her mother came from the aristocratic von Braunschweigs family, but died before Dorothea left Germany to escape the gathering Nazi regime. She soon became one of the family and stayed until she started training as a children's nurse. In September 1939, she was working as a nursery probationer at Chicksands Priory nursery, Bedfordshire. As a German, the government classed Dorothea as an 'enemy alien' and she had to apply for an exemption from internment, which she was granted following a tribunal in November 1939. I don't know where she went after Chicksands was requisitioned in 1940 and served as a Royal Air Force Y-station from 1941, intercepting German air force Enigma messages for the codebreakers at Bletchley Park.

Dorothea and I remained good friends until she died in 1966 of cancer. I felt lost without her and still do, but I have remained in close contact with her daughter, Hella, whom I consider an adopted niece even though she and her family live on Barra in the Outer Hebrides.

In January 1938, the sky was lit up in the red and green glow of the aurora borealis after a solar storm and the residents in Richard's Castle gathered outside to take in the wondrous site. Mrs Randall from the village said, 'Ooh. Argh. Something terrible's goin' to happen.' The following year, she took great pleasure in saying, 'I told you so.'

CHAPTER 5

COOKING OR FIGHTING?

The war changed many lives and mine was no exception, although it affected us in the country probably much less than those in the towns and cities. There was more to eat and while we often heard enemy planes passing overhead, we were spared the horrors of bombing raids that devastated other towns and cities. We did see the flashes of light beyond Clee Hill as bombs fell on Birmingham over fifty miles away. Between April 1940 and August 1943, Birmingham became the third heaviest bombed city in the country.

Like so many of their peers, my parents had first-hand experience of war with Mother's time in Germany and my father's time with the Royal West Kent Regiment during the First World War. He joined up as an army officer from Rochester King's School in 1914 and served in Mesopotamia (a region in Asia covering southern parts of Syria, Turkey and most of Iraq) and India, returning to the UK in 1918 where he found more sedate employment at Lloyds Bank. He remained an active member of the British Legion and was part of a British Legion Police Force mission to Czechoslovakia, as it was known at the time of his mission in 1938, until it was aborted within weeks.

My parents hoped never to see another war in their lifetime, but they got on with life with their usual stoicism and Father joined the Home Guard on its formation as the Local Defence Volunteers on 14 May 1940. Prime Minister Winston Churchill changed its name to the Home Guard two months later. It brought together the men who, through age, occupation or health, were unable to join up and my father was keen to do his bit. As an officer in the Home Guard, he had a large area to oversee on the Herefordshire, Shropshire and Worcestershire borders. At least he had extra petrol ration, but of course we could not use it unless we happened to be going where he was on duty! For both my parents, contributing to the war effort was their duty and they supported my decision to abandon my domestic science course and join the ATS. Later, during a visit home, my father observed my Intelligence Corps badge. I am sure he understood what it meant and knew not to ask. We never had the chance to talk about it, but I hope he was proud.

I filled in the ATS application form on 25 August 1941 and sent it to the Birmingham ATS recruitment office. It seems that I was embarrassed to simply say I was a student of domestic science. Instead, I recorded my occupation as 'Student of Music, Language and Domestic Science', which was, in fact, a better reflection of the skills I had to offer.

Nine days later, I was enrolled in the ATS. I had forgotten I had selected the option of 'Driver' as my first choice on the application form, especially as I did not know how to drive at that stage and certainly did not have a licence. My second selection was 'Specialist', to which I added in the blank space provided 'knowledge of German'.

My call-up papers arrived shortly afterwards with instructions that I report to No. 12 ATS Training Centre in Wrexham, North Wales, for basic training. I dressed in my tweed suit and travelled by train from Ludlow on a train so cramped, it was standing room only. As the day vanished, so did our light, because of the blackouts, and it was impossible to see where we were.

The training centre was situated within the Royal Welsh Fusiliers' barracks. Although in the same compound, we occupied separate areas from the men. I was 'embodied' on 12 September 1941, meaning I was now a full-time member of the army and underwent a series of medical examinations and various anti-viral injections before being issued with the standard kit:

* 3 identity discs and buttons
* 1 khaki cap and cap badge
* 2 khaki serge skirts
* 2 khaki serge jackets
* 4 khaki shirts, 3 ties and detachable collars
* 1 woollen ATS jersey
* 3 pairs of ATS knickers, 3 ATS brassieres and 3 vests
* 4 pairs of ATS stockings
* 3 pairs of shoes (flat lace-up beetle crushers), 1 pair of canvas shoes and 1 pair of laces
* 2 belts
* 1 great coat and 1 anti-gas cape
* 1 pair of knitted gloves
* 2 sets of pyjamas
* 2 towels
* 1 toothbrush
* 1 hairbrush and 1 comb
* 1 brass brush, button brush and a shoe brush
* 1 enamel mug
* 1 each of knife, fork and spoon

* 1 'housewife' sewing kit
* 1 respirator (gas mask)
* 1 satchel
* 1 steel helmet
* Disposable sanitary pads
* Anti-gas items: 6 eye shields and 2 ointments

The list is taken from a signed 'ATS Clothing and Equipment Record' I have from later in the war, so there may be some variation with the number of items in my original basic kit, but this gives a good illustration of what we had to pack into the kit bag.

I do remember that there was a short supply of skirts on my first day at the training course, so I had to wear my tweed skirt until new stock arrived. I must have made a curious sight on parade to anyone watching. Aside from this embarrassing start, I enjoyed wearing the uniform, even though it wasn't a very good fit.

Unlike the WRNS uniform, the ATS one wasn't designed by a fashion designer with the silhouette of a woman in mind. Instead, Jean Knox, the new Director of the ATS in 1941, decided on the modifications to our uniform. The skirt was shortened, the jacket pockets became less bulky and a new belt at the waist helped make the jacket less boxy. Except for the belt, the new changes were more about reducing material usage, rather than for style, and the uniform remained a poor fit. Lady Mary Spencer-Churchill referred to the ATS as the Cinderella of the services partly because of the drab khaki uniform. Another reason for the ATS' lower status in the eyes of the public was a perception that the army required women to do traditional roles – cooks, cleaners, clerks, etc. This led to poor sign-up rates. A survey into public perceptions of the ATS in 1942 led to a change in advertising to appeal to women looking for more interesting postings.

I enlisted two days after Lady Mary Churchill arrived at No. 15 ATS Training Centre at Aldermaston in Berkshire and wasn't directly influenced by her endorsement of the ATS. However, the press reels of her taking part in drills during her basic training reportedly led to a surge in enlistment (and shortages of kit). In 1945, the ATS received the ultimate endorsement when eighteen-year-old Princess Elizabeth joined up as a driver. She even managed to look regal in a khaki boiler suit.

It is impossible to talk about the ATS uniform without mentioning the khaki knickers. They were a sight to behold and not designed for me, measuring in at five feet four and a half inches in height. They had not been subject to Jean Knox's uniform modifications, which was unfortunate because the skirt had been shortened. This meant the knickers either peeped below my skirt or if pulled up, the waistline ended under my armpits. Neither option was desirable nor practical and my knickers became a daily battle to manage.

A collar and tie were a totally new experience for me. I kept pulling on the tie to relieve the painful red mark around my neck, but it was like breaking in my heavy army shoes and eventually the material softened, allowing the sores to heal. Learning how to do up a tie took ages, but I wasn't the only one who found this a challenge. We helped each other out with much laughter and were soon experts at getting dressed in record time.

The gas mask was heavy and cumbersome compared with the civilian models. The rubber mask was connected to a metal canister by a length of flexible tube, which was kept in a canvas bag worn across the chest while the gas mask was in use. At other times, the gas mask had to be carried in a canvas bag across your shoulder. If I ever thought joining the services would make me look glamorous, like the women in the advertising posters, I was sorely disappointed. Nonetheless, I was proud to wear the uniform, especially the ATS insignia and, later, my Intelligence Corps badge.

We were housed in wooden huts equipped with standard-issue military beds, with a shelf each and a lockable chest at the foot of our beds. It was functional, but not very comfortable. Life in barracks was a complete culture shock for me. Girls from all walks of life rubbed shoulders, all learning to work as a team, all with a common purpose – to serve our country. They were young, vibrant and very modern. It seems minor in the chaos of our lives, but the biggest shock came from viewing the girls' behaviour and, in particular, their varied standard of table manners. Until that point, I had naively believed everyone lived as I did.

The barracks became our home for the six weeks of basic training in marching, drilling, parading, cleaning, lectures and tests, until we were finally assessed by female drill sergeants for intelligence and trade assignments. It was exhausting and I fell into bed each night at 'lights out'.

Pay for a Private was ten shillings and six pence per week (twenty shillings to a pound), which doesn't sound much, but we went to the cinema and were able to buy toiletries, including a little lipstick when one could find such rare items. I didn't wear much make-up, so didn't feel the loss of these sorts of items and with shortages in everything, it wasn't that easy to spend your money.

Some of my tasks were also an education. I remember I was given the unpleasant task of looking for lice, something I had never heard of. Those of the new recruits who were found to have lice were bandaged in paraffin-soaked head scarves, but with so many girls living in close quarters the battle over head lice was not so easily won.

I particularly remember the gas mask drill, where we were taken to a small room while wearing our gas masks and a small amount of gas hissed into the room. We were then ordered to remove our gas masks and within a breath, everyone convulsed in a fit of coughing and spluttering as the gas entered our lungs. It was a horrid experience, but taught us the importance of carrying our gas masks at all times, taking gas warnings seriously and obeying procedure without question.

The quiet life in rural Herefordshire and home schooling had not equipped me for anything in particular beyond being able to communicate in reasonable colloquial German. My abandoned college course had only equipped me for running a family home, so I arrived in Wrexham with no true understanding of what my skills were. It was an interesting time to find out exactly what I could put my mind to. I enjoyed the experience of my basic training and at its end I waited with trepidation to see which trade I would be assigned to. Every recruit was assessed and allocated a trade, but not for me a posting as a cook, orderly, store woman or driver, as I had requested on my application form. I was given the seemingly dull trade of clerk on 28 October 1941.

When I told my parents this news, Mother half-joked that I should tell my commanding officer about her ill-health if I did not want to continue. She rarely mentioned her struggles following her operation some years earlier, yet didn't hesitate to suggest it as a 'get out clause' on compassionate grounds should I need it. Like all mothers waving off their daughters, she would have worried about where I would end up, especially as my next movement order directed me into the main target city for German Luftwaffe bombs.

It was a bit of a scramble to pack my belongings in my kit bag and make my way to London. The trip entailed an overnight journey on a train heaving with people, with no space in the compartments and only pockets of space in the corridors. I rolled up my great coat for a pillow and lay in the corridor as best as I could for most of the journey. As there were no lights, it was difficult to see those around me. The night train trundled along slowly, so what a relief to arrive at Euston at 6.30 am, deposit my kit bag in the left luggage office and find a Lyons Corner House to ease a growling stomach. I chose porridge from the menu, but it didn't taste as good as the oats cooked overnight in our Aga into a creamy mixture at home. Of all the experiences that day, the quality of the porridge in the Lyons Corner House has stayed with me when so much has been forgotten, perhaps it was one of the most familiar events of my day.

It had been four years since the whirlwind tour of London in 1937 with Uncle Cecil and Elisabeth Paul, but London still managed to look very grand, despite the bomb damage. By today's standards, there were few people, apart from military personnel, and very little traffic, but it was still the busiest, noisiest place I had ever seen. It seems ironic to me now that my first visit to the capital was on route to my travels in pre-war Germany, where I had received so much hospitality, and my second visit was part of my duty in the fight against Germany.

CHAPTER 6

THE TRAIN TO BLETCHLEY

It is about two miles from Euston to Devonshire House and a straightforward walk, if one keeps to the main Oxford and Regent streets, then onto Piccadilly and asks for directions to The Ritz. Devonshire House was on the corner of Berkeley Street and Mayfair Place, overlooking Green Park and that famous hotel.

When I arrived at Devonshire House, I still had no idea why I was there. I followed someone through a series of corridors to an office, where I sat across from a very pleasant twinkly-eyed army major from the Intelligence Corps. He never introduced himself, but made me feel at ease. He asked questions in German for the majority of the short interview and asked general questions about my family. He never explained why he was testing my German. Perhaps he was just following orders and did not question why. He also asked how I would communicate with someone in Scotland, to which I responded I would do so by telephone, in writing, by telegram or by courier. I had presumed he would have known and asked about my time in Germany in 1937, but it wasn't mentioned. He did not tell me why I had been ordered there, nor what was expected of me. It seemed a strange interview with no discussion about my skills, so the decision about my deployment may have been made based on my tests at the ATS training centre, this interview merely serving as a final check of my intelligence, language skills and reliability.

I must have been deemed suitable because I was given a new movement order to go to Euston railway station immediately and take a train to Bletchley in the Buckinghamshire countryside. On the way out, the army officer led me towards the exit and muttered, 'This is such a labyrinth, you'll never find your way out.' I've always remembered his word 'labyrinth'.

It may seem strange that I just followed my instructions without question and without knowing my destination or the reason for the journey, but this is what I had been trained to do and did so willingly, without any trepidation. It has always been my attitude to take everything in my stride.

I was given a rail warrant, which was a pre-printed typed form with my name, army number and destination handwritten into blank spaces, which I was to swap at Euston for a rail ticket. I collected my kit, obtained my ticket and enquired about the next train to Bletchley. The *ABC Railway Guide* from later in the war shows there was a train approximately every hour, so I would not have had too long to wait between trains if they were on time. Understandably, war caused many delays and cancellations to the trains due to bomb damage and problems obtaining spare parts. While I waited, I probably took the opportunity to get something to eat. After all, I had no idea where I was going, never mind the next time I would eat.

I boarded the outbound train and found a seat with another ATS girl, Winifred 'Wynn' Josephine Angell, a fair-haired woman born in June 1915 in Bordeaux,

France, to British parents. As we began to talk, we discovered we were heading to the same place. Neither of us knew where Bletchley was or what we would find there when we arrived. Trains ran on reduced timetables during the war and were often rammed with people, so it is quite extraordinary that Wynn and I found ourselves seated together.

Wynn wasted no time in describing her dramatic escape from Brussels, where she had lived with her mother, when the Germans invaded Belgium in May 1940. She believed that she had secured her exit with a visa to transfer from the Brussels branch of International Harvester, an American-based manufacturer of agricultural and construction machinery, to the London branch. She remained at the London office until she found work as a secretary at the French Consulate General in Scotland, but then returned to England to join the ATS and use her fluency in French to contribute to the war effort. She told me about her older boyfriend, Georges Dobrynine, who she described as a 'White Russian'. I had no idea what that was at the time, but later discovered this meant he had fought against the Bolsheviks and been expelled from Russia. With such tales, the hour-long journey flew by. Luckily, the train guard announced the station, or we would not have known where to get off.

It was late by the time the train pulled up at Bletchley Station and we disembarked onto an unlit platform, taking care not to fall or get trampled in the dark. In the early months of the war, a first aid station at Paddington Station reported over 200 injuries to passengers getting on and off trains in the blackout. In my experience of navigating pitch-black train stations, I am surprised the figure is not higher.

We would have asked for directions in the station building and hauled our luggage along an enclosed path until we came out beside a guarded gate. The guard took our names and we waited. Baffled women with suitcases and kit bags arriving at the Bletchley Park gates with no idea of what to do next were probably a frequent occurrence for the guards. Author of the memoir *Cracking the Luftwaffe Codes: The Secrets of Bletchley Park*, Gwen Watkins describes arriving at Bletchley Park in similar circumstances as a WAAF recruit. The guard at the Bletchley Park gate on duty that night had a little mischief in mind when he told Gwen she had arrived at 'the biggest lunatic asylum in Britain'.

Our greeting was much more forgettable and I only remember someone arriving with a vehicle and whisking us away to a billet about six miles north, to a village called Bradwell. We arrived at the billet tired and hungry and ready to sleep. After a brief introduction to a pleasant couple, we ate a bite of food and climbed the stairs to our room for the night. The couple's children shared one of the three bedrooms to free up a room for us. We didn't mind sharing, but it was a shock to discover we had to share a single bed. Wynn and I looked at each other with embarrassment and looked at the bed with longing. Neither of us wanted to sleep on the floor, so we made the best of it.

CHAPTER 7

BLETCHLEY PARK

It was October 1941 and I awoke in a strange bed, in a strange house with absolutely no idea why I was there. Wynn and I got ready and caught the coach on the main road, as instructed, and travelled for half an hour with thirty or so people to Bletchley Park. I seem to remember the bus dropped everyone off within the gate.

Everything about our arrival is a blur of unfamiliarity. I thought the house to be a very ugly muddle of red brick, sandstone, timber and an odd copper dome weathered to a blue-green patina. Now I see it through more sentimental eyes. Some people referred to the Bletchley Park house as 'the house', while documents refer to it as 'Main Building', and an American architect who served there during the war called it a 'maudlin and monstrous pile'. To me, it will always be 'the Mansion'.

My next clear memory is sitting in a small office next to the library opposite an army captain with a gun resting on the corner of the desk. He indicated towards a document and said I was obliged to read and sign it on the spot. I had never heard of the Official Secrets Act, but he quickly brought me up to speed. In short, any and all information we read or heard within Bletchley Park must NEVER be discussed outside the department we were assigned to and not for thirty years after the end of hostilities. I could not even tell my parents. The punishment for breaking my silence was severe, the most serious for acts of treason being the death penalty. Treason! What would I be doing that could put me at risk of committing treason?

It was a jolting experience and although specific details about the captain's facial features and the room have blurred in my mind over the years, his insinuation remains vivid and the memory of the gun resting on the desk beside him remains very clear. I did not know how to conduct myself, I am sure I barely uttered a word at first, in fear of doing or saying the wrong thing.

In August 1939, the first wave of Bletchley recruits arrived to find a makeshift set-up of trestle tables and chairs squeezed into the Mansion and outbuildings. The previous year, Admiral Hugh Sinclair had identified it as a suitable location to move the Government Code and Cypher School and the Secret Intelligence Service (SIS) staff to in the time of war. It had been on the market for some time and an advertisement for the sale of Bletchley Park featured in *The Times* in May 1937, with another two months later describing it as suitable to be used as a school or offices as it was in close proximity to a railway junction at Bletchley Station. Hubert Faulkner purchased a number of lots of the estate in April 1938 with a plan to develop it into housing, but after a brief start on the housing, Admiral Sinclair sailed in and purchased a part of the grounds, including the Mansion, for £6,000.

Faulkner's services were retained to oversee the construction of wooden huts and the first huts were in position before Prime Minister Neville Chamberlain announced over the wireless that 'this country is at war with Germany' on 3 September 1939. The initial influx of 137 people, including 50 members working on constructing our codes, exploded to 674 names on a staff list dated 2 December 1940, with 575 of those named at Bletchley Park.

When I joined in October 1941, it did not yet feel overcrowded, the grounds in front of the Mansion resembled a pleasant park, there were spare seats on fewer buses and little in the way of a queue waiting for refreshments. I never wandered further afield than my route from the entrance to the Mansion at first and had little idea of the scope of the construction of the huts. According to the book *British Intelligence in the Second World War* (Abridged Edition), staff numbers rose to about 1,500 at Bletchley Park and its outstations by the end of 1941. This surge can be attributed to an increase in resources made available to Bletchley Park by order of then Prime Minister Winston Churchill, who had taken over from Neville Chamberlain in May 1940. He had visited Bletchley Park shortly before I arrived and seen first-hand how the codebreakers planned to increase their successes against the German Enigma code. Following the visit, four frustrated codebreakers wrote a letter dated 21 October 1941 to Mr Churchill to say he '…ought to know that this work is being held up, and in some cases is not being done at all, principally because we cannot get sufficient staff to deal with it. Our reason for writing to you direct is that for months we have done everything that we possibly can through the normal channels, and we despair of any early improvement without your intervention.'

The authors were to become big names within the history of codebreaking, Alan Turing, Gordon Welchman, Hugh Alexander and Stuart Milner-Barry. Their letter set out four points covering one point for each of the services and a more generalised complaint about management.

Winston Churchill stamped the letter 'Action This Day' and it became the turning point in the fortunes of the Government Code and Cypher School.

In the early days, the main recruitment was of the 'professor types' to do the clever codebreaking and the 'right sort of girl', with good family connections and language skills or a university degree to work as linguists and clerical staff. Of course, that was a starting point and it soon broadened its recruitment to anyone who could be found who fit its unique staffing requirements.

One of those recruited in 1940 was Margaret Julia Mary Lydekker, known by her middle name, Julia. I didn't know her while we were at Bletchley Park; we became friends in Washington at the end of the war in Europe. Although she wasn't the debutante type recruited from London, she lived in nearby Leighton Buzzard with her parents, the Reverend Lionel Lydekker and Mrs Julia Mabel Lydekker at The Vicarage. Looking for work, Julia responded to a local advertisement in 1940.

Julia wrote an unpublished memoir about her time during the war, which offers parallels and contrasts between our experiences at Bletchley Park and the Pentagon, and I have therefore quoted from it in this book. Whereas my recruitment is similar to the thousands of service women who were earmarked for Bletchley Park at their training camp, Julia's recruitment reflects the path of female civilian recruits through the Labour Exchange and an interview by a member of staff from the recruiting ministerial department, mostly the Foreign Office. Julia wrote in her memoir about her arrival at Bletchley:

In the summer of 1940, the time had come for me to decide whether to join up in one of the services or do something else.

As it happened, there appeared in the local paper a rather vague advertisement for clerks/typists required to work at an unspecified government department at Bletchley Park. I had no idea what it entailed, but as my parents lived only seven miles away and just one stop on the L.M.S. railway, this seemed a possibility. I had just finished a crash secretarial course and had somehow managed to acquire some R.S.A. certificates to indicate that I knew more or less what I was doing, so sent these off with some other references with my application and awaited results. To my surprise I received an immediate reply asking me to be on Platform 1 of Bletchley Park Railway Station on such and such a day. This struck me as a bit odd, as my interview turned out to be. I was met by an aged 'Colonel Blimp' type person with whom I passed the time of day. He then asked, 'You were at Cheltenham Ladies College, you can type and you know a little German?' To which the answer was, 'Yes.' So he said, 'That's fine. Report to the main gate at Bletchley Park next Monday and ask the man on the gate to direct you to my office,' which I did. That was it!

During a subsequent interview with an MI5 officer, Julia was quizzed about the political leanings of her clergyman father and her grandmother. I don't recall being questioned about my family's political views. Perhaps my father's service in the First World War and his work with the British Legion were already on record. Julia signed the Official Secrets Act, but makes no mention of the threatening presence of a revolver. She was employed as a Temporary Clerk Grade III on a weekly salary of £2 a week, *'which, never having earned anything before, seemed a small fortune'*. It was four times my weekly salary as a Private in the ATS. My pay was less because my accommodation and food costs had already been deducted along with a small amount put into a compulsory savings account. Julia had to pay her mother housekeeping to cover her rent and food, so our disposable income would have been similar.

So 'fate' led us to the Government Code and Cypher School for the duration of the Second World War. We were two of the thousands drawn from our universities, three services, ministries and local population, all working on the painstaking process of breaking the various codes of the Axis powers to discover their countries' military moves and intentions. We were a team of trustworthy individuals who had an important job to do, even though at the time we did not know the full story and 'small fry' like me did not ask! With the promise of money in our pockets and the prospects of secrets, we set about the work.

CHAPTER 8

A MANSION OFFICE

After signing the Official Secrets Act, I was taken up the stairs and to the right to one Major Tester's department. Wynn was whisked off into a neighbouring office to work in the registration and traffic section, although I did not know that until years later.

Major Ralph Tester's section was based in a set of three or four rooms above the ballroom and overlooking Hut 4. They were fairly small and possibly had been servants' quarters or the nursery in the time of the former owners, the Leon family. There were four wooden desks squeezed into the room I shared with three men and the only other item in the room I remember is an open fire.

I remember two of the three men I shared an office with – Edwin Alfred George 'Tubby' Roots, a Company Sergeant-Major, and Sergeant Clement Albert Le Masurier, from Jersey. I do not recall the name of the third man, even after looking at a staff list. I was recently shown a photograph of Tubby, a portly gentleman with a cheeky smile and glasses, but once again my memory is blank because I can only picture him wearing a gas mask. Every Wednesday morning, Tubby relieved the most unpleasant twenty minutes set aside for the weekly gas mask drill with his rendition of 'In the Mood', which came out as a most hilarious bubbling sound.

A staff list shows that in July 1942 there were fourteen men working in Major Tester's section. Sergeant Le Masurier isn't listed, so may have already moved onto Air Section by that time. Lieutenant Jerry Roberts, who joined the section at twenty years of age in 1941, is listed and remembers the two other codebreakers and linguists in the section. Lieutenant Peter Ericsson was a dashing and very easy-going character whose career at Bletchley Park mirrored Jerry's to the day, from their army promotions to section promotions to shift leader. Captain Denis Oswald was ten years their senior and their opposite in character. He was always sharply dressed and fastidious in his tasks. Jerry recalls he routinely sharpened his pencils, then laid them out in a neat row ready for the day. I did not know Jerry at the time, but had the pleasure of meeting him and his wife, Mei, at numerous veterans' events at Bletchley Park in later years and we became friends.

We were employed by the Government Code and Cypher School's Military Section, under John Hessel Tiltman, an army officer with an extensive military and civilian career in codebreaking. He joined the King's Own Scottish Borderers in the First World War and was awarded the Military Cross for leading a charge to capture two machine guns in 1917 in the Battle of Arras. He was wounded three times, including an injury to the chest that plagued him all his life. He trained as a Russian linguist in 1920 and spent two weeks attached to the Government Code and Cypher School, formed a year earlier from the British army's MI1(b) and the Admiralty's Room 40 cryptographic units. His two weeks translating Russian diplomatic messages turned to a year, after which he was stationed at army headquarters in Simla, India, with the task of reading Russian diplomatic messages as close as possible to the time they were transmitted between Moscow, Kabul and Tashkent. While serving in India between 1921 and 1929, he retired from the army with the rank of Captain and continued with this work as a civil servant. When the new Military Section was set up at the Government Code and Cypher School in 1930, he was put in charge and his army rank of Captain restored. He was promoted to Lieutenant Colonel in September 1939 and promoted to Brigadier in 1944, as well as Deputy Director of the Military Wing. As history knows him as Brigadier Tiltman, or 'The Brig' as he was affectionately known, I have referred to his Brigadier rank throughout for consistency.

The Brigadier preferred to stand while he worked on solutions to new problems with intense concentration, and then move onto the next problem. A humble man, with an ability to turn his hand to any unbroken codes, he made initial breaks into several of the codes of the sections he managed. One of which was the German police code, which he broke in late 1939. He was relaxed about military discipline and rules, but held training in high regard and was well liked by those who worked with him. His office was near ours, not that I had any reason to go in to see him.

The Military Section at the Government Code and Cypher School was part of No. 4 Intelligence School (4IS) and controlled by MI8. A separate section dealing with the wireless telegraphy became No. 6 Intelligence School (6IS), which merged with the Traffic Analysis section in 1944 and became SIXTA.

Wynn and I were posted into the sections responsible for non-machine military ciphers, with sub-sections dealing with German, Japanese, Russian and Italian, as well as other sections. Wynn was in Lieutenant (later Captain) Alfred Shiner's section, which dealt with the registration of the intercepted messages and analysis of the traffic.

I was taken to Major Tester's German Police Section, a small section breaking non-machine hand ciphers of the German military police, SS and German army and air force low-grade codes. At this time, he was a Second Lieutenant, but was promoted to the rank of Major later. However, I have been referring to him as Major Tester for so long, it is impossible to call him anything else. He was a nice, fatherly man who spoke perfect German and was engaged in translating at a very high level, particularly as he was also an expert in idiomatic German.

My duties were registering details from the enciphered messages as they came in from the Y intercept stations, either by despatch rider or teleprinter. I painstakingly wrote the date and call sign for each message on an index card and placed them in date order into the shoeboxes on the desk. This was the only part of the message 'in the clear'. The rest was simply groups of five letters or figures, which was the meat of the message for the codebreakers. I found this rather boring at the time, but realise that all the less interesting tasks were vital because so much intelligence could be deduced from patterns and groupings.

Once the codebreakers deciphered the messages, the translators went to work translating and transcribed the message, although those tasks sometimes overlapped depending on the size of the section and the inclination of the codebreaker. The intelligence officer extracted intelligence about the enemy's order of battle and identified the current location of the troops. They were also able to identify where the troops had moved from on a specific date, based on the call signs, frequencies and the body of the message. There were periods where the traffic analysis and intelligence were done in Hut 6 and Hut 3 by liaison officers placed within those sections. At other times, the section was self-supporting and managed all the tasks within the section. To me, it was just endless numbers and dates on index cards. The intelligence was then forwarded appropriately to the Prime Minister, various ministries and commanders in the field.

I wasn't the only member of the ATS working within Major Tester's section and I imagine we were split over the various shifts. A staff list from July 1942 shows three other ATS on the staff: Sergeant C.W. Wheeler and Privates H. Lipman and M.I. Maunsell. I was pleased to see Wynn (under her married name of Dobrynine) is listed as one of three ATS in Mr Shiner's section.

We worked a shift pattern 8 am to 4 pm, 4 pm to midnight and midnight to 8am. Sounds easy, but it was tiring! I did not work the night shift very often and so found it very difficult. One night I remember I could not keep my eyes open, so I lay on the floor in my great coat for warmth and used my arm as a pillow. These sorts of things happened. Bletchley Park was such a unique experience with many stories of unusual practices because of the nature of some of the staff and the demands of the work. We were all doing what we could to get the work done. I have heard stories that some senior codebreakers in other sections at Bletchley Park had camp beds in their offices for just this sort of thing.

It helped that Brigadier Tiltman was not a rigid military man, as discovered by a recruit, Private William Filby, who recalled reporting for duty in 1940 with a vigorous stamping of his feet and a salute next to the Brigadier's desk. He called Private Filby 'old boy' and questioned the need for army boots. From that day on, Private Filby wore his uniform with white running shoes.

There was an unwritten rule that whoever sat closest to the fire in the office, kept piling on the wood during night shift. I never seemed to be on fire building duty, so my desk must have been the farthest away. The wood never lasted through a cold night, so I often wore my great coat for extra warmth; I found it very difficult to return that coat after the war. As the ATS issue stockings provided no warmth (socks weren't part of the uniform) it was hard to stay warm when one's feet were freezing. The air in the room was thick and claustrophobic with blackout blinds and four bodies in close quarters, but that, at least, provided additional heat, especially when the fire was down to its last embers.

After working with Major Tester for some time, he invited me to take a test to see if my German was good enough to be of use, presumably with translations. I was not hopeful because my German had mostly developed through conversation, but I was pleased for the opportunity to relieve the monotony of writing on index cards all day. After the test, he gently said my German was NOT good enough, so I continued to sort and register the Morse code messages, which came in vast quantities each day. It is said that we received many thousands a day and over time more staff arrived to cope with the volume. We could never have managed alone.

In a very small room next to mine worked a Lieutenant Colonel Francis Sinclair Thompson, who came into the office one day and introduced himself, asking if I was any way related to Rex Vine-Stevens and told me how he served with my Uncle Rex in the Royal Engineers during the First World War.

The first floor of the Mansion was not only home to the Military Section. Julia Lydekker was in Air Section, although we did not know one another at this time, and it is strange to think that I don't recall ever bumping into her or Wynn during our time in the Mansion. In her memoir, Julia remembers her office before the section moved to one of the newly constructed huts:

I was ushered into what had either been a nursery or maids' bedroom upstairs at the back of the house where five or six girls were busy typing away and I was sat down at a table in front of a typewriter with a pile of W.T. (wireless telegraphy) traffic and told to type it like this and that etc.

They were low-grade messages and had no connection with Enigma. They were tiresome to type because did you: a) go across the page typing the three-letter groups and then go back to type in the decoded work or letters underneath, or b) do it all in one, which those who can type will realise meant turning the carriage of the manual typewriter up and down ad infinitum. It was slow, tedious work, but we had a jolly time with a nice fire in the grate in the winter and discovered that, with one exception, none of us really knew an awful lot about typing, which was reassuring. We had the odd report or letter to type, but that went to the one who knew what she was doing while we plodded on with our W.T. traffic.

After a while, with the increase of staff, space became at a premium and a programme of building was put in hand. The upshot of this was that we left our nice snug bedroom and found ourselves in a type of Nissen hut, where we froze in winter and boiled in summer. Furnishings were pretty stark, although I had acquired a very comfy kitchen chair, which I managed to keep with me throughout my time at Bletchley while most others had 'chairs folding flat', which were unspeakably uncomfortable.

I had no idea what I was doing for some time, but eventually discovered what it was supposed to be and also the fact that I was in the Air Section and therefore the traffic was from the Luftwaffe. One was never told anything about what was going on – and one never asked.

The Air Section was under the command of Josh Cooper, who Julia describes as a brilliant mathematician who:

…was apparently completely mad and frightened us all out of our wits. He was a big man with very black hair that fell all over his face, wore round black-rimmed spectacles and had a habit of walking along deep in thought clutching his right ear with his left hand. The corridor down the centre of Hut 10 was very narrow and if from one end you saw Josh approaching you scuttled into the nearest doorway. As he was so deep in thought, he would not have seen anybody and probably knocked us flat. If walking outside, he was to be seen hopping on and off the kerb by the edge of the road.

In her memoir, Gwen Watkins also recounts that Mr Cooper could reach over his shoulder with one hand and interlock all ten of his fingers behind his back. She remembers her future husband once teased Mr Cooper by asking him for the time while he was in this position and was told to ask someone else. Another amusing story related how Mr Cooper would throw his cup into the lake when he did not know what to do with it. This story has become a well-used example of the sort of eccentric behaviour of some of the dons at Bletchley Park. However, Gwen Watkins, who also worked for him, believes this only happened on one occasion. How our memories can trick us over time.

While Josh Cooper is portrayed as a mad professor, written memories of Major Tester have been few and far between until recent years. This is something that has always saddened me, because he was a kind and benevolent man.

Ralph Paterson Tester was born on 2 June 1902 in Kent. After qualifying as a chartered accountant, he moved to Berlin to work as an auditor for Price Waterhouse. Through his travels he met Sigrid Matilda Laurell, a chemist with the Swedish Shell Company, and the couple were married on 19 July 1930 in Stockholm, returning to Berlin afterwards to live where he began working for Unilever. The couple had a son and daughter in Germany, but with the threat of war, Major Tester sent his family ahead of him to England. Meanwhile he travelled home by train through Czechoslovakia, where a group of refugees convinced him to deliver a small notebook to the Czechoslovak Refugee Trust in London. The refugees were removed from the train and the train searched at the border. The Major was fortunate the notebook remained concealed because he later discovered it contained details of Czech communists.

By the end of September 1939, the couple were living in Wimbledon in a large semi-detached house. He continued to work for Unilever at the company's offices in Blackfriars, London, and also volunteered as an Air Raid Precautions (ARP) warden. By 1940, Major Tester had joined the Government Code and Cypher School, where he is listed on the full staff list dated 2 December as a civilian in Hut 5. Upon joining Military Section, he was given the rank of Lieutenant and promoted to Second Lieutenant in the Intelligence Corps on 23 January 1941.

A MANSION OFFICE

Jerry Roberts worked with Major Tester from 1941 to the end of the war and remembered him as an affable chap who smoked a pipe. His skills lay in the German language and in management, leaving the codebreaking to others. He had the ability to get the best from his staff with quiet encouragement, although the battle was already half won with his knack for selecting the right candidates to fill specific posts. Codebreaker Donald Mitchie wrote about Major Tester in a collection of essays called 'Colossus: The Secrets of Bletchley Park's Codebreaking Computers' about his time at Bletchley Park. He was impressed by Major Tester's controlled focus in the office, which was a complete contrast to what was described as Pan-like animality on the tennis court after lunch.

In 1940, a new Axis-power high-speed teleprinter code was discovered and Knockholt Intercept Station began collecting its traffic. Brigadier Tiltman began working on the new code and made an initial break in 1942 using a long message of 4,000 characters sent the previous year. Due to an error, the message was resent and Brigadier Tiltman was able to line up the messages and the differences where words had been abbreviated in the second message using binary arithmetic. Bill Tutte, a chemistry scholar and mathematics enthusiast, was given the deciphered message and a collection of the other coded messages and was able to work out how the machine worked without seeing the original machine.

The machine was the Lorenz SZ (Schlüssel-Zusatz, meaning attachment). Its enciphered traffic, called 'Fish' by the British codebreakers, was sent between Hitler and his commanders in the field by encoding teleprinter messages through the attachment. It was a brute of a machine and devilish to break, with ten

54

wheels to encipher a message and two drive wheels. A new section under Major Tester, the Testery, was set up to tackle the Lorenz code by hand methods, using information about the starting position of each wheel. This was determined by machine methods in another new department called the Newmanry, after the first head of the section, Professor Max Newman. Colossus, the first programmable computer built by Tommy Flowers, of the Post Office Research Station at Dollis Hill, was invented as a method to find the wheel settings.

A number of the codebreakers from the Police Section were transferred into the Testery, including Jerry Roberts, Tubby Roots and Corporal Jim Walford among others. I had no knowledge of where they had moved to and knew not to ask. I would later see them around Block F, where Colossus was installed in 1944. I once saw a group of men wrestling with an enormous piece of machinery outside Block F and can't think what else it could have been other than Colossus. Jerry, for one, was delighted to move onto something challenging and engrossing.

Meanwhile, I continued to register the ever-increasing number of messages on index cards in the German Police Section while the department expanded around me and the work carried on. But soon it would be my turn to move into more challenging work, which changed the course of my war.

CHAPTER 9

THE GERMAN POLICE SECTION

Breaking the Enigma code is the prevailing story of Bletchley Park and rightly so. Major Tester is best known for his work in the Testery breaking the Lorenz teleprinter cipher used to connect Hitler with his high command. These high-value codebreaking feats also commanded the most attention and resources during the war. Due to the strict compartmentalisation of our duties at Bletchley Park, I had no inkling of the purpose of my daily tasks or the arterial network pumping decrypts and intelligence around Bletchley Park, so I never heard the word Enigma or Lorenz. As well as machine codes, the Axis powers used hand ciphers to send messages or, like the German police, they used both, reserving their most secret and ruthless messages for Enigma. Even then, the Germans considered some information to be too sensitive to send by wireless and sent it by courier. Hut 6 handled the German police Enigma traffic sent by the SS on the keys codenamed Orange I and II and Quince keys at Bletchley Park. Orange I was used for administrative information including the daily counts at concentration camps and weather reports. Some of the messages on this key were also sent by hand cipher, which helped the codebreakers break into Orange I. The SS used the Orange II key to send messages between Berlin and divisions on the Eastern

Front. Orange II all but disappeared in 1942 and the SS introduced Quince for messages about the administration of all SS divisions.

The Government Code and Cypher School had success with these non-machine ciphers, which included those of the German police and army, and air force low-grade ciphers tackled in the German Police Section at Bletchley Park under Major Tester. It was author Michael Smith who revealed to me the nature of the work carried out in Major Tester's section almost seventy years after I sat down for the first time at the desk in the small office in the Mansion with a stack of index cards and a shoebox beside me.

The German police force was a complex organisation under Heinrich Himmler, as the *Reichsführer* of the SS and chief of the police. He oversaw the brutal protection squads, called *Schutzstaffel* (SS); the security service (*Sicherheitsdienst des Reichsführers-SS* or SD); the security police (SIPO), which was divided into the criminal police (KRIPO) and the feared secret state police (GESTAPO); and the German Reich's uniformed police force (*Ordnungspolizei*, known as ORPO). High-ranking SS members held key positions in all these organisations.

The ORPO used a Double Transposition hand cipher as its primary source of communication, which was the focus of the German Police Section. This cipher was later replaced in 1941 by another one called Double Playfair, which used a square of letters set out over five columns and five rows to encipher the message. Once enciphered, the message is enciphered a second time on another 5 x 5 square. This method was replaced by Raster in September 1944. The codename used by the Government Code and Cypher School for the German police cipher was

'Domino'. Messages were processed through the German Police Section, but traffic analysis and intelligence reports were at times carried out in conjunction with Huts 6 and 3, but at other times the German Police Section was entirely self-supporting, with all elements of the codebreaking process managed within the section.

When ORPO began to use an Enigma key in 1944 for its most classified messages, called Roulette at Bletchley, the messages went to Hut 6 for deciphering and processing. The other German police organisations relied upon the unbroken TGD Enigma key, also known as the Gestapo key and named TGD at Bletchley Park after its fixed Berlin call sign even after the call sign changed. TGD was used for the most important German police messages and was never broken at Bletchley during the war, but they used hand cipher for some of their other messages. The SS used the hand cipher sparingly, preferring to use Orange I, II and III, and Quince keys.

The German police used fixed call signs at the beginning, which were allocated to regional areas, and any of the police organisations within that region could use the call sign. This differed from other German defence forces, such as the army, where the series for changing call signs and frequencies used for transmitting the messages was allocated to specific groups and sub-sections within that group, and only those groups could use the call sign, regardless of their location.

Berlin was the main command in the police network, with sub-control stations that had their own group of minor stations. The minor stations could only contact their designated sub-control on a set frequency, and the sub-controls could communicate with each other on another frequency and contact the command station in

Berlin. Police and SS formations on military action against partisans also used the same links.

The preamble at the start of the messages intercepted at the Y-stations followed the format: place of originator, serial number, time of origin, number of letters and address, followed by text in five letter groups, with the discriminant included in the first group. All this information told the message recipient who had sent it, over what frequency and how to read the message. Changes to the format occurred in March 1942. Then later that year, the place name was replaced by the call sign. Understanding who was using each call sign meant that Y intercept stations could, among other things, sort out messages identified as important, collate them quickly and efficiently, and then send them to the codebreakers. I recorded the call signs and the date on the index cards and I had no idea what happened to the messages once they left me, other than they ended up in storage in the depths of the Mansion at the end of the process incase one had to be retrieved for re-examination. Traffic analysts could make intelligence deductions from these details without decoding the messages.

The deciphered German police messages did not offer much tactical information to help Allied forces win the war, but they did reveal information about the impact of the war inside Germany, based on reports about daily attacks on railways, heavy raids on factories and towns, the movement of millions of evacuated people from East Germany, the movement of police regiments, and the organisation of short-wave traffic between Berlin and principal towns. Other messages reported an outbreak of typhus and details of Hitler's expectation that cowards of both sexes be hanged with labels attached to the corpses to identify them. They also reported the location of stolen art treasures and the movement of rice and butter. One only needed to read the names SS, SIPO and Gestapo to realise that some of the content of the messages included statistics about the mass extermination and imprisonment of Nazi Germany's enemies. As the Germans considered this information more sensitive, most of it was sent using the Enigma keys, but some of it was sent using the hand cipher, particularly from the Russian front. Another reason for deciphering the police traffic was to see if the messages were resent over other networks for the army or air force. Words used in one message could be used as cribs in another.

Two codebreakers have written about their time in the German Police Section and provide technical descriptions about breaking the code. In his book *Lorenz: Breaking Hitler's Top Secret Code at Bletchley Park*, Jerry Roberts summarised his year spent breaking the Double Playfair cipher in Major Tester's department before he moved onto the Lorenz teleprinter code in the Testery during the summer of 1942. Another codebreaker, Noel Currer-Briggs, wrote about his time in the German Police Section in *Codebreakers: The Inside Story of Bletchley Park* and describes a test set up in a Bletchley Park hut to simulate breaking Playfair, Afrika Korps and Abwehr traffic in the field. He and three other sergeants from Major Tester's section were part of 107 Special Intelligence Section (later 7 Special Intelligence Company) attached to 1 Special Wireless Group sent to North Africa breaking Double Playfair codes in the field.

The History of the German Police Section in Appendix 1 has more detail about the section's achievements.

Before the war, Captain Shiner worked on the German police, army and air force low-grade codes, as did the French and Polish codebreakers. The number of messages on the police network at that time was between 80 and 100 messages a day. The French gave the Government Code and Cypher School a diagram of the internal German and Austrian police network in 1938. By 1943/44, there were police networks in Russia, Poland, Czechoslovakia, Holland, Norway, Yugoslavia, Italy, France and Romania.

The German Police Section within the Military Section began in autumn 1939 as a section of about twelve shortly after Brigadier Tiltman made the first substantial break into the system.

Picking up the traffic in Great Britain was difficult and successful interception depended on other Y-stations scattered widely across the country, but many of these intercepted the crucial Enigma traffic. The French at Metz had no problems picking up the medium frequency traffic, so a group of codebreakers and clerks went to France in December 1939 under the codename 'Mission Richard', after its head Major Richard Pritchard, to set up a collaboration with the French. The team settled at the French headquarters at La Ferté-sous-Jouarre, although in the beginning most of the French regarded the mission as a rival, rather than as a friend. Despite this initial wariness, Mission Richard was a success and expanded in February 1940 when another officer and twelve other men travelled to France, leaving behind a traffic section within the German Police Section at Bletchley Park to send the English-intercepted traffic daily by bag. The French worked on the even days, while the Mission Richard team worked on the odd days. Major Pritchard returned to England in spring 1940, confident the collaboration was breaking all but the occasional day's code helped by the German's use of messages of identical length.

On 10 May 1940, the so-called phoney war came to an end when Hitler invaded Belgium, the Netherlands and Luxembourg on the way to France. The 'dramatic appearance of Capt. Tozer in travel-stained mackintosh and a whirl of cold night wind late on the 10th' alerted Mission Richard to the invasion. Work began to falter and then stop, as Mission Richard retreated with the French. Records were destroyed and the team left the French GHQ at Ussel to travel to Bordeaux, then returned to Bletchley Park safely, but empty-handed.

In the three months it took for the section to get back into production at Bletchley Park, the Germans had not made any changes to their police codes. Harpenden, Denmark Hill and Home Forces Unit (Y3) became the main intercept stations for the German police Domino network, and several of the staff from the traffic section moved to the intercept station.

In 1941, Winston Churchill gave a speech that could have revealed the source of information and the Germans may well have been listening. On 13 September 1941, Chief of the German Order Police Kurt Daluege sent a message to his superiors in the SS and the police in Russia:

The danger of decipherment by the enemy of wireless messages is great. For this reason only such matters are to be transmitted by wireless as can be considered open ... Confidential or Secret, but not information which is containing State secrets, calls for especially secret treatment. Into this category fall exact figures of executions (these are to be sent by Courier).

New security measures soon followed, with the introduction of Double Playfair at about the time I joined Major Tester's section. It replaced the Double Transposition cipher, but it turned out to be easier to break, although still not straightforward. It is likely I was recording the dates of these messages and the operators' call signs, on those white rectangle cards in my office in the Mansion. According to the history of the Police Section:

This was the point at which the most considerable increase of staff was required, for there was no reason now why three keys should not be broken daily and three sets of decodes issued. The training school at Bedford was able over a period of 2 or 3 months to meet the need of the cryptographers, but the need for clerks in the traffic sorting and decoding department was harder to fill since the numbers required were larger and the claims of other sections in BP equally great or greater. This is perhaps one of the most important and surprising lessons learnt in the development of a highly specialised organisation such as BP – that it is much easier to get together the skilled part of the train than the unskilled.

In July 1942, some of the team moved into the Testery to begin the work on the Lorenz cipher, removing a number of experienced staff from the section. In September of the same year, the Germans replaced the fixed call signs for regions with a more irregular system and two months later began to use six Playfair squares changed every two hours. Additional security measures included moving addresses and signatures to within the body of the message. However, the Bletchley Park codebreakers had been recording on index cards the habits and traits of each station, so even though these measures slowed down the codebreakers, by February 1943 the section was producing four to five hundred decodes a week. In October, over 3,000 messages were deciphered and seventy keys broken. As the number of broken German keys increased, each one was labelled with the name of a card game.

In February 1944, Enigma traffic, codenamed 'Roulette', was being used by high-ranking police officials and was picked up on the police network. This was broken regularly using messages sent on the Double Playfair cipher, which were duplicates of messages sent using the Enigma key (known as re-encodements). These messages included statistics relating to the horror of the Holocaust. However, Double Playfair was then replaced by Raster and all breaks from re-encodements dried up. Raster was a more secure cipher and caused a serious setback to the progress of the section, to the point that, according to the *History of Military Sigint*, Raster 'had now reached a point at which further exploitation would have been uneconomical without the enlistment of high-grade machinery'. As a result, Roulette was rarely broken until there was a breakdown in German police wireless security towards the end of the war. These two ciphers were difficult to break, but the human error made it possible with enormous effort.

The successes in the German Police Section in breaking the majority of the ciphers, proved the section's worth as a training ground for new codebreakers before they moved onto other codebreaking challenges. In summing up, the History of the German Police Section states:

The contribution of the German Police Section to the war effort was not of the sensational kind. Its task, when the lights went out in Europe, was that of peering unremittingly into the gloom, and of lifting a corner of the blackout here and there. But the results, even if not of the kind that make headlines, and history, were certainly such as Intelligence staffs came ultimately to value almost as much: the kind of information that, piece by piece, builds up a background of knowledge upon which decisions can be based.

CHAPTER 10

LETTERS AND TELEPHONE CALLS

After the security talk on my first day at Bletchley Park, realisation hit – I was 'cut off'. My family could not visit to check I had settled in and I could not tell them where I was posted. They may have feared I was in London after my last instructions sent me to Devonshire House, so I could only reassure them all was in hand in the event of an emergency. As instructed, I gave my family and friends PO Box 222, Howick Place, London as my permanent address.

The sender could send me a letter or a parcel, but the post office drew the line at handsome Canadians arriving at the sorting office expecting to surprise their girlfriends as my boyfriend, John Sancton, discovered to his embarrassment. He arrived in London without the knowledge that the address written in our correspondence was not my billet address. He arrived to come face to face with a bemused post office clerk refusing to pass on further information about where letters to the postal address were sent. I know he was not the only one to fall into that trap. Whereas the clerk in Howick Place ushered John away, another incident led to a breach of security in Bletchley.

Entering the Post Office at Bletchley Station in October 1943, an officer enquired about the address given by his relative as PO Box 111. The clerk directed the officer to Bletchley Park, where the officer must have approached the guard at the gate and asked for his relative. The guard asked to see the officer's papers, which were all in order, and reported the incident to Bletchley Park's security officer, who reported it to Deputy Director of Bletchley Park Nigel de Grey.

Nigel de Grey left his work in publishing to join the Admiralty's Room 40 codebreaking unit, where he became a first-class codebreaker during the First World War, being part of the team of codebreakers to break the German 'Zimmerman' telegram of 1917 proposing an alliance between Germany and Mexico, the contents of which influenced the United States to join the war. In August 1939, Nigel de Grey's fluency in French and German was once again needed in the Government Code and Cypher School's naval section before moving to head up the Intelligence Exchange Section. As part of his role as Deputy Director, he managed the breaches of security, some of which are recorded in a file in the National Archives. Compared to some in the file, the lack of discretion by the postal worker is minor so Mr de Grey wrote to Mr Wilkins, the head postmaster at the Bletchley Post Office to remind him, the 'Post Office should not disclose the identity of a Box number, and I shall be grateful if you would bring it to the attention of your clerks, that they are not to tell anyone that Box 111 is in fact Bletchley Park.' A chastised Mr Wilkins apologised by return post for the lapse in the clerk's judgement.

PO Box 111, Bletchley, had been in use from the earliest days of the war, when there was a total ban on disclosing Bletchley Park's whereabouts. The secrecy did not last, as I discovered when looking around an exhibit at Bletchley

Park and a photograph of an original notice dated 21 February 1940 caught my attention. The notice removed the restriction from those at Bletchley Park to conceal the whereabouts of the area. Staff could receive letters, parcels and telegrams to their billet address. They could post a letter at the local post office, where the sorting office would stamp Bletchley and the date across the top. Telephone calls were no longer restricted to the kiosk in the Mansion, so those lucky enough to have a telephone at their billet could use it. Those who did not have a telephone could use the local call boxes.

The Government Code and Cypher School did not abolish all restrictions; everyone was still bound to secrecy about the nature of their official activities. The notice also states that the 'official designation of the establishment will, in future be "Government Communications Headquarters"; this should be sufficient explanation for the curious to account for presence of personnel from so many different Government departments.'

The PO Box address continued, which was useful in the event of a sudden change to billeting arrangements. The PO Box 222 address appeared on BP Order 25, dated 17 April 1942, as an option as a permanent address and a requirement in correspondence to foreign nationals (aliens) and to addresses abroad (including all of Ireland). Letters or parcels bearing this postal address could not be posted locally, but must be posted in London or in the box in the Mansion hall marked 'Letters to be posted in London'. The mention of Bletchley or any indication of the location of the war station was not permitted in letters abroad or to foreign nationals. From the date of the order, billet addresses could be used in all other circumstances and letters could be posted locally.

Telegrams could also be despatched locally, under the same rules as letters. I still have a copy of a telegram I sent to my father, something one only did for a special occasion, or in an emergency. The cost of a telegram up to July 1943 was nine pence for up to nine words, then one pence for each extra word. There were additional fees for sending on a Sunday, priority posting or using an 'artistic' greeting design, which was chosen from templates. I chose a colourful floral design in a gold envelope for Father's birthday telegram. From July 1943, the cost to send a standard telegram soared to one shilling (twenty pence) for up to nine words and one pence thereafter.

Two years later, BP General Order No. 32, dated 7 April 1944 (two months before D-Day), shows another change in the rules. The mention of Government Communications Headquarters was no longer allowed; use of this descriptor was for official purposes only.

It is astonishing to me that the stringent rules of those early days became more relaxed once staff numbers grew, while the codebreaking successes reaped ever greater benefits for the commanders in the field. If the enemy ever got a whiff of what was going on, the repercussions would have been unthinkable, yet Order No. 32, makes for an interesting read:

LETTERS:
1. *The address Bletchley Park is not to be used in any circumstances; neither is Government Communications Headquarters which is reserved for official correspondence.*
2. *Billet addresses should, wherever possible, be used.*
3. *Those who write abroad (but see para. g below as regards Prisoners of War etc.) or who for any reason require a more*

permanent address are advised to use the address: Box 111, Bletchley, Bucks.

4. *Letters so addressed will be delivered to Bletchley Park and distributed from the office to the addresses. In order to facilitate delivery, the Block or Hut number and Room number may be added after the addressee's name, <u>but the title of the Section must not be stated</u>. Own initials should be given in full; the use of nicknames or husband's initials will inevitably cause delay.*

5. *Service personnel accommodated in Service Camps or Quarters must comply with the instructions issued by their Commanding Officers.*

6. *Letters, parcels etc., received with instructions to collect postage on delivery will not be accepted.*

7. *The letter box in the Main Building is for the posting of letters only. No responsibility can be accepted for parcels (even if stamped at the letter rate) or letters which will not fit in to this letter box.*

Letters to Prisoners of War, Internees, and Residents in Enemy Occupied and Neutral Countries:

a. *The Censorship Authorities have forbidden the use of Post Office Box addresses in these letters. Home addresses should be used. If this is not possible, billet addresses should be used. For those residents in the B/P Hostel, this will be: 2, Wilton Avenue, Bletchley, Bucks. And for those at Drayton Parslow: Drayton Parslow Hostel, Bletchley, Bucks.*

b. *Letters may be posted locally or, for those who so wish, they can be posted in London if they are sent to Miss Henderson, Registry, Block E, with a slip pinned to them requesting this to be done.*

c. *No mention is to be made of Bletchley Park, or "The Park" or "BP" itself in your letters; nor of anything that would* convey that there is a large or important Government Office in Bletchley.

d. Both for the safeguarding of the work and for the sake of the well-being of the prisoner of war, be particularly careful to make no reference to our work of any kind whatever. Letters to prisoners of war are closely scrutinised by the enemy to obtain information about the Allied war effort and if they deduce from open or cryptic references in a letter that the prisoner of war has information to give, they will not hesitate to try and extract it from him by any means that they think likely to be effective.

e. For the same reason all references to anything connected with HM forces should be avoided and no person serving in the forces should be mentioned and no photograph of anyone in uniform should be included.

f. There is no prisoner of war air mail service to the Far East and no enclosures whatever are allowed in letters to prisoners of war and civilians in Japanese hands.

g. Post Office Leaflets F2880E and P2327B containing full G.P.O. information on correspondence with prisoners of war may be obtained at Post Offices.

h. The same precautions must be observed in letters to internees and residents in enemy-occupied and neutral countries, as letters to enemy-occupied countries certainly and letters to neutral countries probably will be scrutinised by the enemy.

i. Correspondence with residents in enemy-controlled territory can be transmitted only through such an agency as the Red Cross organisation, and is to be limited to communication with relatives of the writer in urgent circumstances. Particulars of the special facilities available can be obtained from the local Citizen's Advice Bureau.

j. In matter of doubt, questions should be addressed to the D.D. (1), Mr de Grey, Room 18, Main Building.

TELEGRAMS:
The telegraphic address "Bonzo, Bletchley", may be used as an
alternative to billet addresses. Whether "Bonzo, Bletchley" or
Box 111, Bletchley is used, the Block and Room number may be
included in the address. The office telephone number is not to
be used for telegrams. Telegrams received with instructions to
collect charges will not be accepted.

TELEPHONES:
The telephone number Bletchley 320 may be given to next of
kin and to billeters for use in emergency. It is not to be given
to anyone else. The telephone exchange has been authorised to
monitor calls, and if the privilege of using the official number
is abused, the privilege will be withdrawn. Calls from Ireland
will not be accepted.

Commander Bradshaw updated the General Orders as
necessary, some only annually. His office distributed a
number of copies to each section, which were shared with
the members of that team. A copy may have been put up
on the noticeboard in the Mansion, which was a strictly
controlled affair. Items had to be approved and initialled
by the Establishment Officer before they made it onto the
noticeboard. The watchmen overseeing the communal
area would be checking for any illicit notices posted on
the board. Each section would have also had its own
items for the eyes of the section only, and more general
orders distributed to the sections from Mr Bradshaw's
office may have been posted here too.

With so many rule changes, I was careful to confine
the content of the letters to my parents to social chatter
about the activities we got up to in our spare time. There
was always something to say about music and I would

enquire about my favourite animals, the goats. Letters aside, I was actually more likely to call them directly from one of the telephones in the Mansion located beside the stairs. It was easier to fill a telephone call with general chatter, especially when there was a limit to a few minutes, and listen to the voices from home. As more people arrived and the blocks appeared, more telephone boxes appeared across the park, each with its own set of rules. An order from Commander Bradshaw dated 10 April 1944 details the procedure for using the telephones:

Telephone Boxes are provided in the Main Hall, Main Building; in the Main Hall, Block D; in the Main Hall, Block E; and between Blocks A and B. All private calls must be made from these boxes.

Boxes 3 and 4, Main Building, are to be used for local calls, that is to say, calls covered by the South Midland and Bedford telephone directories. These two boxes are connected to the Bletchley exchange and are fitted with G.P.O. money boxes. Local calls may be made at any time.

Books are kept in each Box (except 3 and 4, Main Building) and anyone making a call is to insert name, section, telephone number called and charge for the call. For local London calls, the charge is 2d. The operator at HQ London will inform the caller of the amount of a toll or trunk call before this is put through. The caller must then put the correct amount in the money box.

Private calls through London, which will be strictly limited to 3 minutes, may as a general rule only be made before 9 am, between 1.30 pm and 2.30 pm, and after 6.30 pm.

Any calls outside these hours must be authorised to the Telephone Supervisor by Heads of Sections.

After 6.30 pm, owing to congestion on the line between B/P and Broadway due to private calls, which necessitates the employment of extra operators, no-one will be allowed in future to make more than three individual calls per week, except in cases of extreme urgency. This restriction does not apply during other permitted hours.

It was hard to keep up with all the rules, so it is hardly surprising I only used the PO Box 222 address. It seemed to be the safest option or maybe those in the services were required to use that address, much in the way they would use the unit address in the field. Imagine my surprise to find at least one occasion where I wavered on this rule, which I discovered while looking at documents for my travel to Washington in 1945. I am astonished to discover that on a form for entry into Baltimore I wrote 'Shenley Road Military Camp, Bletchley, Bucks, England' as my address. At least the incident occurred after the war in Europe had ended, and I was violently ill during the journey so wasn't quite myself, which is ironic because my sickness was a mixture of travel sickness and my fear of giving the game away!

CHAPTER 11

BILLETS

I knew I had landed a jammy billet the moment I entered the home of the Foxley family, Salisbury House in Loughton. The previous billet had been agreeable, but crowded with a family of four and three billeters in a three-bedroom house. I am sure the family was relieved to be rid of us, but it was likely a short reprieve before a new billeter arrived wide-eyed, awkward and desperate to be polite. It was a constant battle for the billeting officer to find sufficient housing for the ever-increasing staff and find it at a reasonable distance from Bletchley Park.

Salisbury House was a large nineteenth-century cottage with sash windows and a spacious rear garden. It was home to Mr Percy Foxley, a railway clerk with the London Midland and Scotland Railway, Mrs Ethel Foxley and their children, Wilfred, Beryl and Donald. Donald had been a clerk on the railway before being conscripted in 1942 and serving as a driver mechanic with the Northamptonshire Yeomanry.

The village of Loughton was very rural in those days and approximately four miles northwest of Bletchley. It was less than two miles south of my previous billet in Bradwell, so I was on the same bus route into Bletchley. It may have only been one less bus stop along the route, but it was three extra minutes in bed in the morning and three minutes saved in the journey back to the house after a long shift.

My move to Salisbury House must have been somewhere between autumn 1942 and the following spring. Wynn left to have a baby in September and moved to Melrose Road in Pinner near London. I was sad to see her go; we had been together since the beginning, but she was close enough in London for me to catch a train and pay her the occasional visit.

I know I was settled in Salisbury House by April 1943, because the date is scribbled on the rear of a photograph taken outside the house. It is the only one I have of the time I spent at Bletchley Park and is one of a handful of photographs I have of the war years. I am seated on a chair in full uniform with a blanket thrown over my legs and I am laughing at something to the side beyond the camera's view. Barbara Brown, another of the three ATS billeters at the house is sitting beside me in her ATS uniform, but is not wearing a jacket. It must have been a warm spring day, because Barbara is in her shirtsleeves, although I am well wrapped up, so clearly I was not feeling any warmth from the sun. Barbara has thrown up her arms at whatever has amused us and the fact that she is holding a writing implement while a book rests in her lap reminds me she was a graduate of one of the colleges for women in Cambridge. Barbara left at some point, and we didn't keep in touch and another girl moved into her room.

With the ration books for three ATS billeters added to the family's rations, Mrs Foxley was able to cook excellent meals and bake cakes on the old farmhouse range next door. The meals were supplemented with the fruit and vegetables the Foxleys grew in their rear garden, so there was plenty of food for us all. It made eating with the family preferable to eating in the canteen at Bletchley Park.

The government had issued some economising tips in a booklet, *Economise on Fuel* issued in October 1941, which encouraged neighbours to share their cookers to save on fuel and to have hot baths at night, rather than during the day. This was difficult if we were on night shift. Furthermore, we were not to use any more than five inches of hot water, and soap was rationed in 1942, although shampoo powders and shaving soap were not. Even the King had every bath in Buckingham Palace and Windsor Castle marked at five inches in 1942, but I am sure they weren't the tin baths we experienced in the kitchen at Salisbury House. The Foxleys were considerate of our privacy and left the house until we had finished our bathing. I imagine the dirty bathwater was put to good use on the vegetables, just like at home.

It felt like a luxury to have a comfortable bedroom to myself after sharing one since joining up. The room was furnished with a bed, wardrobe and a washstand, because there wasn't a bathroom in the house. It was outside at a reasonable distance, although not as far as the lavatory at Ryecroft. I was rather anxious during my first visit to their lavatory because there was a pile of Baptist hymnals beside the toilet; I wasn't sure if I should use them or read them.

Mr and Mrs Foxley were quiet, homely and very religious. They treated us with kindness and I became very fond of them. Even after I moved into the Shenley Road Military Camp in 1944, I went round to visit them and I have a photograph from 1950 when I visited them after the war. It is likely they would have received new civilian billeters as soon as we were through the gates at the new camp, because accommodation was still in short supply and moving to the camp freed up billets within the surrounding area, so it is likely their next guests were civilian recruits.

I sometimes went shopping with Mrs Foxley to Wolverton or Towcester. We got on very well and I was happy to go with her when I wasn't off with a friend on my days off. I could only travel home to Herefordshire occasionally, because it was terribly expensive, and I needed more than a weekend's leave; the journey each way took most of the day. I only managed a day trip for my twenty-first birthday. I was home long enough for a slice of sponge cake, then had to set off back to Bletchley a short time later.

Mr and Mrs Foxley were never the sort to ask us about our work, which Mr James Bellinger, the security officer at Bletchley Park, concluded in a memo to the operational head of the Government Code and Cypher School, Commander Alastair Denniston on 23 March 1941 was the status quo among residents of their generation:

In accordance with your instructions, I have to report having made enquiries relating thereto, and I herewith submit for your information, particulars of my observations.

During the course of my investigation I have visited nearly every hotel, public house and club in Bletchley and the surrounding districts, and I have associated with persons drawn from all walks of life, some of whom I know personally, and it is as a result of my conversations I have had with them, I am able to mention the following –

First, I am satisfied that most of the older inhabitants of Bletchley were at one time very anxious to know what sort of business was carried on, at the "Park". They knew it was some sort of Government establishment, where a number of Naval, Military and Air Force Officers, and civil servants were employed, but I do not believe that any information as to the nature of the duties undertaken has been imparted to them.

The greater majority are very patriotic, and their curiosity having died down, they go about their own affairs satisfied that whatever is done, is all for the good of the Country.

Things were different when Admiral Sinclair first purchased the site for his war station in 1938. The local gossip about a government office purchasing it for ARP was hot news, especially when the newspaper reported a statement from the Air Ministry stating it had been purchased for the air defence of Great Britain. Local residents scrambled to the newspaper stalls for more information about the mystery of Bletchley Park. Demand for news was so high the newspapers sold out and *The Bletchley District Gazette* published an apology in the Saturday edition on 4 June 1938 to all its disappointed customers who had not been able to purchase a copy. The newspaper used it as an opportunity to encourage readers to fill out a subscription form.

The mystery deepened a week later when the newspaper printed another reply from the Air Ministry, which stated there were no plans for an establishment at Bletchley Park and it was possibly the War Office. Leslie Hore-Belisha, the Secretary of State for War, replied to the local MP's queries that the War Office had no plans for Bletchley Park. Not an auspicious start for a secret site hoping to keep a low profile. Four years had passed since the speculation began about the purpose of Bletchley Park and the security officer's reconnaissance in the local establishments suggested that, for the most part, many locals had settled down and were getting on with their own lives.

I stayed in touch with Donald Foxley after the war, speaking to him regularly on the telephone and visiting him in Loughton, where he lived all his life. During a visit a few years ago, my friend asked Donald if he had ever been curious about the new faces he saw in the village and local area. He said he wasn't curious, just pleased to see so many pretty girls at the bus stop.

He had his mind on enjoying himself while on leave because life in a tank was hard work and terrifying. In June 1944, he was deployed in Normandy and fought through France, Belgium, Holland and Germany in a Sherman tank. He saw horrific scenes while in France that were hard to forget

The Foxleys treated me very well and it could not be easy for them or any of the families who played host to the thousands of us who were billeted in the area. The billeting officer had a difficult task trying to find billets for the constant intake of staff, which made transport arrangements difficult with so many billets scattered throughout the area and widening the net to include Bedford. Nigel de Grey described the process as 'unpleasant and unpopular, even for the patriot'. In order to retain billets for Government Code and Cypher School staff it was 'eventually necessary to procure "closure" of BP area by Ministry of Health, which excluded other organizations from billeting in the GC&CS reserved area.' And 'The best billeting officer was a revolting type but he got the billets.'

The WRNS were quartered together in large, requisitioned houses from their arrival and officers had their own house, Walton Hall. Wavendon, Steeple Claydon, Crawley Grange and Gayhurst housed as many as 250 at their peaks. Stanmore, Eastcote and Woburn Abbey opened their doors in mid-1943 and quartered much higher numbers, with Eastcote housing 830 WRNS in the week ending 20 May 1945.

Deborah Kennett, my friend from the domestic science course, operated one of the Bombe machines, the electro-mechanical machine designed to reduce the number of possible Enigma settings the codebreakers had to check to find the daily key to read the enciphered message. She worked in Hut 11 and had been billeted with other WRNS at Woburn Abbey. I had not seen her since our leaving Radbrook so it was a delightful surprise to run into her one day in the grounds of Bletchley Park. I occasionally stayed over at Woburn, although I don't remember the procedure for such an arrangement. The palatial house owned by the Duke of Bedford was grand to look at from the outside and surrounded by beautiful parkland, but was stripped of its character inside and freezing cold. It was a rather utilitarian space, only brightened up by the chatter and energy of its inhabitants. It was always a relief to return to my own room after bunking with a group, but before too long, I had to say good-bye to that luxury and move with other male and female army personnel into a purpose-built army camp.

CHAPTER 12

HOORAY FOR THE WEEKLY PAY PARADE

Before the war I had not earned my own money, so it was quite something to have money handed to me each week in the pay parade at Bletchley Park. The ATS deducted my compulsory savings amount and my room and food costs at the billet before handing over the payment, leaving me with money in my purse for clubs, outings, toiletries, drinks and the other sundries one needs within the limits of rationing and shortages of the war.

As a humble Private, I earned 10s 6d a week and more once I was promoted. To get this anticipated weekly pay, we entered a hut near to the Mansion. The easy chatter and laughter between fellow members of the ATS ended at the entrance to the hut. Pay Parade was a serious and formal business, but was a break from the daily grind and a welcomed top-up to our finances.

We assembled in a line 'at ease', facing the officer sitting at a table with our pay. In the silence of the room, we waited and, as our name was called, we stood to attention, marched up to the officer and saluted. Next, we transferred our pay books from our left hand to our right and handed over the pay book for the officer to record the pay for that day. Finally, we received the money with our right hand, transferred it to our left, saluted, did an about-turn and marched out of the room. We had to attend the pay parade even if we were off duty, but I can't recall how it worked when we were on night duty.

While in Chester after the war, I met June Rosina Solloway (nee Collins) from Hut 5. I did not know her while we served at Bletchley Park, but for some reason, I recognised her by the back of her head from the pay parade. We were lined up in alphabetical order and as her name was Collins, she was always ahead of me in the queue. It took some time to get through every other letter of the alphabet before 'V', so I had plenty of time to examine the back of heads. I have no idea what was so memorable about her head, but there you are, sometimes the oddest memories are the ones that stick.

Promotion at Bletchley Park was automatic. There were no tests or interviews beyond our trade tests and our rank progressed so that our pay was comparable with the civilians. The regulations for the pay were set out in the Regulations for the Auxiliary Territorial Service 1941, with a basic daily rate for each rank, plus additional pay. Once I was mustered as a Tradeswoman and became appointed as a Clerk Class II, my wage jumped to the Group C band, with a daily rate of 1s 10d. At this point it is worth mentioning that one pound equalled twenty shillings (s), one shilling equalled twelve pennies (d), a penny comprised two halfpennies or four farthings, while one guinea equalled one pound, one shilling.

Date	Rank	Trade	Weekly Pay
03.09.41	Private	(non-trade)	10s 6d
28.10.41	Private	(Clerk II)	12s 10d
05.11.41	Acting Lance Corporal	(Clerk II)	£1.2s

18.05.43	Acting Corporal	(Clerk II)	£1.3.4d
21.08.44	Acting Sergeant	(Clerk II)	£1.13.10d
15.03.45	Staff Sergeant	(Clerk II)	£1.19.1d

I have assumed any acting rank was paid at the same rate as if it was a full post.

There were additional payments and allowances of:

4d per day for war pay

2d per day for special proficiency

½d for each actual day of service for toiletries, cleaning materials and haircutting

Julia was employed by the Foreign Office as a civilian in 1940 and paid £2 as a Temporary Grade III Clerk. The figures show that as a civilian she was paid considerably more than I was as a woman in the services, but she would have had to pay housekeeping to her mother. For those in the billets, this housekeeping rate was fixed at one guinea and included a main meal. Deducting a guinea from Julia's weekly pay left her with 19s per week as her starting wage.

As an example, the perm I had before going to Washington cost four guineas. A third-class single train ticket to Euston cost 7s.4d and 9s.10d for a return. A third-class ticket from Paddington to Woofferton cost 22s.2d or 29s.9d for a return; or the route I would most often take, Paddington to Ludlow, cost 22s.10d for a single ticket and 30s.8d. I would then have to pay for a taxi from Ludlow to my home in Richard's Castle.

CHAPTER 13

FUN AND FRIENDSHIPS AT BP

The canteen and recreation huts were social places at Bletchley Park, communal areas where we would strike up a conversation with new people and a place to meet friends to arrange visiting the cinema, or going to a dance, or a concert. If I was working on the day shift, I ate my evening meal at the billet, but in the canteen if I was on the evening shift. I rarely did the midnight to 8 am shift, so don't remember the arrangements for that, nor do I remember the quality of the food served at Bletchley Park. However, books about Bletchley are filled with amusing stories about hard peas, a debutante eating the discarded meat from her friend's plate with its additional cooked cockroach and odd concoctions of beetroot and prunes. Julia remembers in her memoir the change in catering from the early, abundant days of her arrival in 1940 to the mass-produced dishes for thousands of people when increased rationing began to bite:

Life was fairly luxurious at that time and we had a first-rate dining room with waitress service and a large choice of meats and game birds or something equally appetising for our lunch. But this delectable food soon turned into soya link sausages and other horrors and finally ceased altogether when a large, uncomfortable cafeteria was built to cope with the number of personnel which were increasing all the time – starting in hundreds and ending in thousands.

Not everyone found the food distasteful; some wrote about it with enthusiasm. I suppose it depended on what you were used to and how you approached it. I was always one to accept whatever was put in front of me without complaint. The number of meals served (breakfast, lunch, dinner, snacks, high tea and supper) increased from just over 10,000 in March 1942 to its peak in June 1944 of just over 32,000. Every week for approximately a year, from March 1942 to the same month the following year, the catering staff prepared 250 meals more than the previous week.

As it is now, food and dining was a social event. Even grabbing a weak coffee in the club in the recreation hut, in Hut 2 or the Mansion, or queuing for the promise of a rare bar of chocolate at the wooden Navy, Army and Air Force Institutes (NAAFI) kiosk was a place to chat, laugh and ease the monotony of the work while you waited. At first, the morning kiosk opened for two hours from 8.30 am to give those coming off the midnight shift time to use it, but staff getting off the morning transport were repeatedly late to their desks because they were queuing for the NAAFI, chatting no doubt. The morning opening time was reduced to half an hour from 8.30 am (later changed to 8 am), but was open for four hours in the afternoon from 1.30 pm (later changed to 1 pm). According to BP Order 30 dated 13 April 1944, army personnel could only use the NAAFI and civilian kiosk if they possessed a BP/NAAFI ration card. I don't remember these at all! I didn't smoke during the war, but a weekly allocation at privileged prices was limited to forty cigarettes or tobacco equivalent to thirty cigarettes and you had best be organised before the weekend, as NAAFI did not sell them on Fridays.

Then as now eating out was a way to spend time with friends and boyfriends, and there were places outside the perimeter fence to visit. I would also go to a restaurant in the main street in Bletchley with friends. I once asked for beans on toast, but as the waitress was bringing it over, she slopped it down the back of my battle dress. What a waste of food.

The Women's Voluntary Service (WVS) at Bletchley Station ran the canteen and served fantastic fish and chips at a good price. It was close to work, so we could nip out and get back for the transport or the next shift. I wasn't the only one to think highly of the canteen and every month the WVS reported it was always busy and more volunteers were urgently needed. Years later someone confessed to sneaking out of Bletchley Park to the canteen to buy cider and cakes. The staff in another section took it in turns to go to the WVS cafeteria each morning for a jug of tea and hot buttered rolls. The cafeteria was so popular it remained open for the entire war, except for one weekend in May 1945 when it closed for cleaning. It was in full swing again on the following Monday and continued to serve up food and drinks for at least another year. Some women from Bletchley Park volunteered to peel mountains of potatoes, including Margaret Rock, a mathematics graduate of Bedford College working as one of the few women codebreakers at Bletchley Park. She was based in the cottage research section from April 1940 under eccentric, veteran codebreaker, Alfred 'Dilly' Knox, who broke the Zimmerman telegram with Nigel de Grey in the First World War. He ranked her codebreaking abilities as fourth or fifth best of the professor types working on Enigma, although she was only graded as a linguist. She followed in the footsteps of her cottage colleague Claire Harding and volunteered in the railway canteen to take a break from the mental strain of work, and wrote to her mother on 13 October 1940 to share her experience:

Claire had told us that you could have anything you liked to eat there, but luckily we had both found time 'to get' something quick beforehand as there wasn't a second when we could have eaten in!

There was no bacon or egg so everyone had sausages and chips, and it was almost one person's job to keep the potatoes peeled as there had been no time to do any ready on the previous shift. Then there were the sausages and baked beans on toast, and the toast burnt if you didn't look! Many of the men are in a rush for their train which are steaming in and out of the station very noisily all the time. The other helpers were very pleasant or rather, one I like very much, the other was rather irritable, I daresay she was tired. They all took turns at everything and of course there was never-ending washing up, which everyone did in spasms when there was a second to spare. Altogether a hectic rush, which was a nice change after much over-exercise of one's brains!

I do not recall meeting Margaret Rock during the war, although with so many people and so many clubs, it is hard to remember everyone. Our paths may well have crossed in the Bletchley gramophone club. I understand she bought a gramophone while in Bletchley, with her mother's encouraging guidance, 'I hope your gramophone will be a success. Don't pay less than

£6-something.' She also played in an orchestra when the retained staff moved as Government Communications Headquarters to Eastcote after the war. Perhaps her gramophone was one of those we gathered round to listen to music.

The music events held at Bletchley Park were my favourites. Concerts were given by the RAF Griller String Quintet and others, the madrigal choir and the gramophone club. Musicals were put on by the Bletchley drama group, along with Bach choir concerts under Herbert Murrill, who was a professional singer and was employed by one of the radio stations after the war.

I became good friends with Second Subaltern Helen Mary Little through our mutual enjoyment of music. She was three years older than me and an inch shorter with grey eyes and mid-brown hair. She graduated from Gosforth Secondary School in Newcastle upon Tyne with a list of qualifications including London matriculation in English, Maths, Latin, German and French at the age of seventeen. Of the languages, she spoke very good German and was fluent in French. In summer 1939, she lived with a French family for five weeks returning home as things were heating up in Europe. A week later Great Britain declared war on Germany.

She studied French and German in an accelerated degree at University College Hull, which took two years to complete, and also completed one term enrolled in a shorthand and typing course at York Commercial School. She worked as a clerk for London North Eastern Railway for six months and a draughtswoman in the Signal & Telegraph Drawing office for five months. The pay for both posts was £2.4.0d a week. She enlisted in the ATS in York on 3 February 1942 under her maiden name

Colebrook and was called up seventeen days later to No. 8 ATS Training Centre. In May, her commanding officer commented, 'Colebrook is now an unpaid L/Cpl at No. 8 ATS TC. She likes the life and her work but is anxious to use her languages as she feels that they will get "rusty" otherwise.'

She was posted to the 9th Eastern Platoon No. 2 London District Group and marched through the ranks being posted to the Intelligence Corps in August 1942. She married Lieutenant D.W. Little at St Stephen's church, Acomb, York on 5 September 1942 as a Lance Corporal and had the rank of Sergeant when she was appointed as Clerk (Intelligence) Class I in November 1942, when she was posted to No. 4 & 6 Units. This may mean she was posted at that time, although the location only states 'F.S.'. She then attended No. 2 Officer Cadet Training Unit in Windsor as a Staff Sergeant and was commissioned in July 1943 and posted to No. 6 Intelligence School (6IS) at the 'War Station' in the Government Code and Cypher School's Military Section with the rank of Second Subaltern.

I remember going to a concert with Helen and listening to Mozart's *Così fan tutte*, a comedy opera about two sisters and their lovers. I made a joke about *Così fan tutte* – how to keep your feet warm, much to our hilarity. The concert may have been in the assembly room on Wilton Avenue or perhaps somewhere within the park, where a makeshift stage was assembled for performances. The ballroom and dining rooms were given over to the recreation club for periods during the war. There was also a recreation hut on the right-hand side of Wilton Avenue on the opposite side of the road to the canteen and just outside the main gate. The recreation club also included clubs for table tennis, dance, badminton, squash, art and a chess club. There was also a lending library and free lectures. In April 1941, the Government Code and Cypher School agreed to install two full-size hard lawn tennis courts at a cost of £500.

The park grounds also formed part of our recreation time. If it was fine weather, we would sit by the lake or walk around the grounds, but I was always circumspect on how far I would wander, never straying towards the other huts or blocks. One year, there was heavy snowfall and people could be seen ice skating on the lake. Although it was forbidden to take photographs, somebody broke the rules, which means images of those ice skaters on the lake can be enjoyed by more than those who were there at the time.

We went out together in London on weekend leave and stayed at Helen's parents' house in St John's Wood. We also enjoyed cycling around the Bletchley area without any plan. There were no road signs, so it was a case of cycle and see where we ended up and hope one of you remembered the way. Eventually, we became familiar with the local landmarks and street layout. It was much more comfortable to leave the uniform at the billet and wear civilian clothes for cycling.

I would sometimes cycle in my best dress if I was cycling to Wolverton to a dance on summer evenings or to Old Bradwell, where there were regular dances at the Memorial Hall in aid of the 'Forces Fund' and which featured an RAF band between 7.45 pm and 11.45 pm. Civilians paid two shillings entrance fee, whereas the service fee was discounted at one shilling. It was only a few miles and cycling was much easier to sort out than a lift. I don't imagine I was the only one; it was a popular mode of transport during the war. I bought a second-hand bicycle while in Bletchley for some princely sum. They were in great demand and tricky to get hold of, which is probably the reason mine was stolen. I contacted the Military Police, but was more or less told to go away as it wasn't a priority (and was probably untraceable). I often wonder who took it. Good luck to them. It was a very basic contraption with an uncomfortable seat, a temperamental wheel and no bell.

I never knew what work Helen was involved with at Bletchley Park and she never discussed it, even after it all came out, not even to her family. Helen's service record cryptically states 'to be Specially Employed. Billeted to Staff Pay' with effect from July 1943 and remains Specially Employed when the No. 4 & No. 6 Intelligence Schools were combined with all Military Section into Military Wing GCHQ. Helen's daughter, Jennifer, shared a few memories about her mother's attitude to discussing her wartime years.

My parents married in September 1942 – Dad always said that officially he didn't know what she was doing but he had a good idea. His regiment was the 1st East Yorkshire Regiment, and he was the intelligence officer for the regiment which I always thought was a strange coincidence. His regiment went over on D-Day but because of his knowledge he was not allowed to go. He eventually went over on D-Day +9 from Dover.

Mum took the secrecy very seriously and even after the books were published in the 1980s, she still said very little. When we were children and asked her what she did in the war, the answer was always the same, 'If I tell you, I'll be shot.' She did come out occasionally with pithy remarks like, 'I sometimes knew what the Germans were up to before the Germans did.'

No. 6 Intelligence School was absorbed into German Army and Air Section in Hut 6 in 1944 forming SIXTA, where Helen worked on traffic analysis. The section was based in Beaumanor Hall until 1942, then Hut 15 at Bletchley Park, before moving to Block G in 1943. Traffic analysis involved, among other things, the study of the enemy wireless network and information from intercepted messages to be able to identify a station from its call signs. It also included the study of volume and patterns in the traffic to determine which networks were the most important priorities for interception, so that the right number of sets could be allocated to intercepting messages on those networks. The analysis covered everything available without deciphering the message. Helen is most likely to have known the full story of Enigma and never felt able to reveal the full extent of her work at Bletchley Park.

Another friend, Deborah Kennett, also became engaged while we were at Bletchley.

The newspaper carried a notice about her engagement to Sub-Lieutenant William Campion of the Royal Voluntary Naval Reserve in 1942 and their marriage in 1944. I attended the wedding, which sadly ended in divorce in 1952, but she remarried happily and became Deborah Vickers. I sometimes stayed with her at her billet in Woburn Abbey and other times she invited me to stay with her parents at 13 Mill Lane, Cambridge. I only remember there were a lot of steps to the house. Memory can be infuriating! We would spend the day going around Cambridge. It was always enjoyable to get out of Bletchley for a time and see new places, especially as it was difficult for me to get home due to the distance and prohibitive cost.

Although we did not have lots of free time, the varied social occasions made it easy to find new friends among others who were well aware of not being able to talk about our work. Things were a little trickier with friends outside of the park. Social dances were one of the activities that would put us in close proximity to those from outside and there were plenty to enjoy locally. Fortunately, I became friends with one of the 230 American servicemen who came to Bletchley Park from 1943, and he made an enthusiastic dance partner.

Walter Sharp was studying mathematics at Ohio State University before the war. When the 6813th first arrived at Bletchley Park at the end of August 1943, it was regarded as part of the US army's Signals Intelligence Division (Signal Section) Headquarters European Theatre of Operations, under the command of Colonel George A. Bicher. By February 1944, the 6813th Signals Security Detachment was established and the last contingent arrived in March 1944, bringing Walter Penrose Sharp to Bletchley. He was billeted in Little Bicknell and we became friends

His American designation was 'Technician 5th Grade' and he worked in the Machine Room of Hut 6, which at that time had moved into Block D.

He also spent two months in the Newmanry, the section dedicated to the statistics of the high-grade traffic by mechanical means, including the first programmable computer, Colossus, and wrote in a letter to me in July 2004 that he 'worked on Colossus for a short time'. He found it frustrating because he claims not to have understood what he was doing and was 'extremely happy' when he was posted back to Hut 6 testing the output of the Bombe machines to find the key needed to read that day's messages.

Walter was five years older than me and born in Newark, New Jersey. He was five feet nine inches, of slender build with blue eyes and brown hair. There was nothing romantic about my friendship with Walter, he had married his sweetheart back home in 1942. It was reassuring to me to have a safe dance partner who made me feel chaperoned rather than courted. He liked having a dance partner who wasn't looking for more than friendship. We could enjoy the hop and other evenings out without worry.

Our evenings were more sober affairs than those he spent with codebreakers Donald Mitchie and Peter Aiken, who invited him on a pub crawl one evening. He remembered little afterwards except the chorus of a bawdy song. Walter headed home soon after D-Day along with his detachment and was discharged from the army on 2 April 1946. He worked for a year teaching maths in an engineering school and afterwards went to work at the National Security Agency (NSA)

I made contact with Walter and his second wife Jean in 2003 and we wrote to each other each Christmas for many years. I enjoyed a visit to see them while in Washington in 2009 as part of a trip to revisit some old haunts.

Most of his letters were general updates about the previous year, but a few contained snippets about his work. We always wrote letters rather than email, Walter once explaining that although he had seen 'the big ones' at the time of their earliest use at the NSA, he never got used to using a personal computer. Walter retired from the NSA in 1973, then worked as an income tax accountant until retiring in 1993. He continued to help the elderly and those on low incomes in the community with their tax returns. He was popular during the tax season and completed thirty-five tax returns by hand for his neighbours in the retirement community. Walter died on 8 December 2013 at the age of 95.

It has been important to me to keep in touch with as many of the people I met at Bletchley Park as possible. Reading through this chapter makes me realise that my enjoyment of the war years was for the most part as a result of the kindness and friendship of others. Many of the friends I made welcomed me into their homes during the much-needed rest days and their families greeted me with hospitality. It eased my homesickness and introduced me to new places and experiences. If I lost touch with those I met at Bletchley, I tried tracking them down years later. Sadly, I lost touch with Helen Little after I left Bletchley Park for Washington and after sixty years of trying to locate her, came across the notice of her death in September 2012. I called the funeral directors and by coincidence, her daughter Jennifer was on the premises at that time. I was staying nearby with family, so was able to attend the funeral. It was such a long way from home and a remarkable coincidence that I was in the right place at the right time. I have stayed in touch with Jennifer and her husband ever since, and they have been my guests on several occasions at the annual Bletchley Park Veterans' Reunion. For those who I did lose contact with, I can at least remember them on these pages.

CHAPTER 14

WARTIME LOVE AND ROMANCE

In 1942, my parents introduced me to a handsome Canadian who served in the Royal Canadian Air Force, John William Sancton. My parents had become embroiled in the matchmaking plan of Lady Cane, the wife of my father's friend Sir Cyril Cane. He had served with Father in India and became Consul-General in Detroit, San Francisco and Rabat. Lady Cane wrote to me and wrote to John as a way of introducing us and we arranged to meet in London.

John had been a reporter for a Montreal newspaper when war broke out and he enlisted in 1940 and sailed to Great Britain in March 1942 to be deployed to a large RAF aerodrome at Biggin Hill in Kent. I do not know the connection between John and Lady Cane, but she seemed to think we would make a good match.

We met in London to see shows and enjoy restaurant meals. He was devilishly handsome with dark hair, a neat line of moustache and dark eyes behind round spectacles. He was charming, great to talk to and fun to be around. We wrote to each other, but nothing about the war effort, of course. He was flying sorties over German-occupied France. Years later his son contacted me and sent a copy of a diary entry marking my birthday on 13 May and noting he had written to me a few days earlier. Another entry he had in his diary was more specific about his morning activity of grenade-throwing followed by choir practice after lunch. It was easy to become attached to him because as well as handsome, he was clever and interesting. As a newspaper man with a way with words, he knew how to court a girl.

Courting, as we used to call it back then, had an extra sense of urgency in the wartime, from making the most of embarkation leave mixed with the worries about an unknown future and couples seemed to rush towards marriage.

Wynn's fiancé was coming to England in March 1942 to volunteer with Belgian forces. She asked me if I would find somewhere else to stay so Georges could sneak into our room and spend the night. We had moved to a different billet by that time. I obliged my friend and found alternative digs for the night. What the couple didn't know was that Georges' entry into the country brought Wynn to the attention of MI5 and a copy of their report is held in the National Archives:

Winifred Josephine DOBRYNINE

This woman, against whom personally there is nothing recorded, first became of interest to us in February 1942 when she was attached to one of the Intelligence Schools. The question whether it was desirable that she should remain in this employment was referred to us in view of her alien fiancé's impending arrival in this country from Portugal in order to join the Belgian forces. The factors which she was engaged; whether she was regarded as discreet; whether she would be difficult to replace; and the security record of Georges the man (sic). In light of very favourable reports received from the Commandant of the School regarding ANGELL's behaviour she was not removed from her post.

Georges DOBRYNINE arrived in the UK in March 1942 and is described as a stateless ex-Russian. He was interrogated at the L.R.C. soon after arrival and made a favourable impression on his examiners. DOBRYNINE appears to have been once a great opponent of the Bolsheviks, having served against them with the White Russian armies in which he was an officer, but since leaving Russia in 1921, he stated that he has never engaged in any political activity. His release from the L.R.C. to the Belgian military authorities was recommended.

Mrs DOBRYNINE was discharged from the ATS for family reasons on 13 September 1942. Her husband was granted extended leave from the Belgian forces in January 1943 and placed at the disposal of the Belgian Ministry of Education. They have not come to notice since.

MI5
15 January 1945

An announcement appeared in *The Scotsman* newspaper announcing Wynn and Georges' marriage on 27 April 1942. I am surprised to see Wynn's occupation is shown as 'intelligence'. It would not take much for anyone who saw the announcement and knew where she worked to come to a conclusion about the sort of work that went on at Bletchley Park. With the extra scrutiny of MI5, any sign of indiscretion on Wynn's part could have dire consequences for her work. The matter resolved itself a few months later when Wynn left Bletchley Park in September 1942 and welcomed a son, Piotra, in early 1943.

The ATS discharged auxiliaries on family grounds when pregnancy reached three months, whether the woman was married or not, so Wynn had no choice but to leave. I was billeted for a short time with another girl who was forced to leave after getting into a spot of bother. A pregnant single woman was frowned upon in those days and it left a mark against her character, but the man did not seem to bear the same social stigma. In peacetime, the government had a marriage bar requiring women to resign on marriage, but made an exception in wartime so a married women could serve throughout the war or until she was expecting a child.

Marriage wasn't high on my agenda, and I did not feel I was missing out as my friends met and married their sweethearts. I had never been away to school or university where I could socialise in my spare time with my peers, and I was enjoying a new independence. Most of my two terms at the domestic science college had been in the infirmary, so I missed out on that camaraderie there. Bletchley was my university and I wanted to enjoy the clubs available to us, dance the night away at a local hop with friends, watch a film at the Bletchley cinema and escape to London for a show and shopping.

All too soon, there seemed to be an unspoken understanding with John about our future, so I invited him to visit my parents at Ryecroft with me. By introducing John to my parents, I could find out if they liked him; they had been a part of the introduction through Lady Cane after all. We enjoyed a pleasant stay, but at some point, Mother took me aside and said she did not think we were a good match. I don't remember if she explained her reasons and I am sure it was no reflection on his character. He was, after all, very charming. It was a blow; I trusted her judgement above all others and trusted she knew me well enough to have a good sense about these things. If I accepted a proposal, should he make one, I would sail away to Canada after the war and that meant leaving my parents and sister behind. It was hard to contemplate living at such a distance with the added burden of Mother's ill health. Canada was so far way it would be impossible for me to get home should I be needed. In the end, I did not feel sufficient spark to put all the other considerations aside. Mother's illness was a contributing factor, but it was also a get-out clause, much like the one she offered when I completed my basic training. In the end I realised that it wasn't that I didn't want to marry John, I didn't want to marry anybody.

John received a commission in the Royal Canadian Air Force at the end of 1942 and was posted to RAF Station Highgate, London. He spent the rest of the war working in intelligence in England and crossed the Channel six days after D-Day to join the forces at Juno Beach. Things worked out for the best for John because he met Mary while in London, where they married in 1945. He returned to Montreal with his new wife soon afterwards and continued with a successful career as a journalist, editor and publisher of *The Westmount Examiner*. He died in 2004 and was survived by Mary, his three sons, his sister and grandchildren. He returned to England once more in 1994 with other Canadian veterans to attend a state dinner in Portsmouth held by Her Royal Highness Queen Elizabeth.

After John and I broke up, I knew I was not on the lookout for love. The war years were a dizzy mix of hard work and lots of social distractions. I had made so many male and female friends and there were lots of events to enjoy. There were dances at nearby American RAF bases, where a bus would be put on to take us to the dance and return us at the end of the evening to our digs. They were great fun because of the lively music and refreshments from the American air force stores for us to enjoy. I remember another similar event arranged close to D-Day, but this time it was a party in a large house loaned for the event, instead of a base. If I remember correctly, the men were part of a unit going abroad the next day. There was dancing, but the atmosphere was a little flat, which is understandable with their imminent departure abroad. So, I took a stroll in the garden with a handsome captain of the Royal Engineers. I don't think I knew his name and it was all very innocent on my part in those days and we were just chatting and walking around the garden without realising we were very near to a pond. Before we knew it, we had slipped and fallen in. I am sure we laughed. We were soaking wet, which made for a damp journey home. I hope his uniform dried out in time for the next day.

When I told my colleagues at Bletchley Park about it the next day, Lance Corporal Jimmy Bentley put pen to paper and made a joke of it in the form of a cartoon in pencil and ink. Jimmy and I were in the neighbouring offices in the Japanese Military Section in Block F by that time. He was a clever man and put together the painting in a matter of minutes using ink we used in the office and gave it a cheeky title 'Combined Ops!' The painting shows a pond surrounded by shrubs and the soles of two pairs of shoes sticking out above the surface of the water making a dramatic splash. One pair of shoes is smaller than the other and you can just see a hint of khaki green trousers above the larger pair to represent the captain. On the bottom of the page, he has drawn two caps with my corporal stripes and three pips below his drawing of my ATS cap. He has also drawn the Intelligence Corps and

Royal Engineers colours as well as a Japanese symbol, but I don't recall what it means. I only remember the incident at all because of the humour in the painting and how quickly Jimmy put it together. It's a cheekier version of what actually happened, but great fun.

Towards the end of the war I met James Douglas Patch, also known as Jimmy, serving with the Long Range Desert Group (LRDG), a branch of the British army specialising in raids and reconnaissance in enemy territory. A member of the LRDG had to be mentally and physically resilient and self-reliant. I met him at the wedding of my friend Enid Hilda Noakes, who worked in the Japanese Military Section. She married a chap who served with Jimmy. Jimmy and I hit it off and we exchanged details and wrote to one another for a short time. He was very handsome with blond hair and boyish good looks.

We must have met towards the end of the war because I had moved to Block F and he was serving abroad until spring 1945. He had experienced quite a war by the time we met, not that I knew it then, of course, but he recorded his experiences for the Imperial War Museum. He enlisted in the Royal Artillery on 16 May 1940 and was recruited as a gunner into the Long Range Desert Group in 1941. He served in Libya in 1942, including Tobruk, and was promoted to navigator. After the enemy surrender in Tunisia in May 1943, Jimmy was told to learn Greek. He then served in Greece in autumn 1943, where he was captured on the Greek island of Levitha, but escaped from the cattle truck attached to a train transporting a group of prisoners of war from Yugoslavia to Germany. As he was special forces-trained, he was prepared for escape with a small hacksaw protected by rubber sewn into his trouser flies, a silk map sewn in his beret and a compass hidden in his collar. It took him five days to saw through the barbed wire sealing one of the corners of the truck. He remained in Yugoslavia fighting with a guerrilla group and returned to England in March 1945.

The other reason I believe we met towards the end of the war in Europe is the presence of his initials and his address in an engagement book I acquired in Washington. His initials are written several times in the early pages so he must have been on my mind quite a bit in those early weeks, but with so much going on we lost touch and that was that.

CHAPTER 15

NOCTURNAL HORN

On 21 October 1944, a newspaper article titled 'Nocturnal Horn' appeared in the *Buckingham Advertiser and North Bucks Free Press* reporting on the court hearing of Joyce Nash, an ATS driver charged with sounding a klaxon horn twice at 11.20 one night in response to a stationary vehicle blocking her way. Miss Nash of Wilton Avenue (likely to be the hostel at the end of the road) was collecting women during the unlit autumn night for their shift at a 'Bletchley public department', the newspaper reported.

Miss Nash appeared at Leighton Magistrates' Court with the Bletchley Park transport manager as support. He explained there was not a central collection point or timetable in smaller villages whereas towns had both, so drivers had to find an alternative way to alert passengers to their location. Knocking on the doors to round up the women had led to complaints. The late-night door knocking and bell ringing did not go down well with families already inconvenienced by losing a room in their house as a billet. The transport manager argued that sounding the horn was not a serious issue in wartime and promised to ensure a collection timetable was put in place for the Leighton Buzzard district. The case was dismissed on payment of a four shilling fine. I do hope the Government Code and Cypher School shouldered the bill rather than poor Miss Nash.

I don't suppose there were too many Bletchley-based departments transporting groups of women for the night shift of a sufficient size to employ a transport manager, so I can only assume the 'Bletchley public department' is a euphemism for Bletchley Park or one of its outstations. Even if it were not related to Bletchley Park, the story illustrates the logistical and physical challenges of getting to work on time for Government Code and Cypher School staff. During the week of the magistrates' court hearing, 115 drivers drove 34,410 miles transporting 29,780 passengers on single journeys, as well as 1,435 despatch runs and 543 luggage runs.

By the time of the newspaper article reporting the court case, I was based in the Shenley Road Military Camp just outside the boundary of Bletchley Park and no longer needed daily transport. When I was billeted in Bradwell and Loughton, it was always a dash to get to the designated pick-up area on time, because the driver did not have Miss Nash's patience and moved onto the next stop without waiting for stragglers.

I was on the same route when living in Bradwell and Loughton. According to a timetable from 1943, the two buses a day dedicated to getting staff to the Park at 9 am and 4 pm stopped at Newport/Bradwell corner and Bradville in Bradwell, then Old Bradwell crossroads, followed by the Triangle Inn in Loughton. There were an extra four stops in Bradwell and two in Loughton for the midnight shift, to reduce how far staff had to walk in the dark. I should point out that I remember the morning shift commencing at 8 am, which is a bit of a puzzle.

Jimmy Thirsk, who worked as a Log Reader at Beaumanor in the Traffic Analysis Section and was billeted near to me in the next village of New Bradwell when his section moved to Bletchley Park in 1942, discovered the best way to find his way along the driveway on a moonless night after evening shift was to shuffle towards the voices of the drivers calling out the names of their destinations. The buses dropped the night shift and collected the evening shift and were on their way once again.

I saw civilian and service personnel on the bus, and I remember one civilian in particular whose face was caked in make-up. She must have spent a lot of money on the products. I wondered about her being so heavy-handed when they were so difficult to get hold off. I never knew her name, but we often chatted away to those sitting next to us without the faintest idea who either of us was. It was just to pass the time, although I was often sleepy on the morning bus and was more likely to look out of the window for the thirty-minute journey. The return journey was dark, so you only saw the person next to you in silhouette or perhaps a hint of more if it was a moonlit sky. We still chatted on, talking about the latest film on at the cinema, when the next dance was going to be, who was going. . . that sort of thing.

One morning I woke up late and threw on my clothes without much thought and dashed downstairs to make a run for the bus. At the bottom of the stairs, I looked down and saw to my horror my long khaki knickers, but no skirt. With haste I did not know I possessed, I retreated upstairs to my room to pull on the forgotten skirt. The Bletchley Park transport had already gone, so I walked for fifteen minutes to catch another bus on the main A5 road.

Julia lived with her family in Leighton Buzzard and had to endure the transport throughout the war.

Initially the train was okay, but with the Blitz it became very erratic and we often got carried past our stop because the porters never knew which was a stopping train and which wasn't (usually the latter). So the 'powers that be' brought in some extremely antediluvian coaches to get us into work. For a while, I travelled in a charabanc with doors down the side and a jolly folding hood that sometimes worked, but mostly didn't and so the rain came through the roof and windowless sides. Luckily, we were picked up outside the local hotel and if our transport was more than an hour late then a senior member of the establishment who happened to be billeted there would take us inside and ply us with ginger wine, which was very restorative. This vehicle collapsed quite soon and we then had some very antique coaches that broke down frequently, usually when one was coming off the evening shift and several times I found myself two miles from home at 1.00 am and having to walk the rest of the way. Later they produced some utility buses with the hardest wooden slatted seats I have ever encountered, but which got us to and fro very successfully.

Julia was not exaggerating about the state of the transport vehicles. The Government Code and Cypher School had to use whatever vehicles were available and 'make do and mend' – and continue to use them until they stopped entirely. A Military Transport Corps Driver Report Book for 1942 held in the Bletchley Park Archives offers a snapshot of the condition of the vehicles and some of the driving incidents. Had I been aware of these at the time, I may have bought a bicycle much earlier and only ever travelled to work by that means.

On 11 March 1942, one D. Graham of the ATS was driving vehicle number 154 behind a large steam lorry. I can only imagine how slow such a vehicle was travelling, but it was slow enough for Miss Graham to overtake the lorry at an approximate speed of thirty-five miles per hour. A car appeared head-on out of the steam in the other direction and they crashed. A police constable arrived to take her particulars. Miss Graham did not sign the entry so may have been injured or taken home in a state of shock.

On 14 March 1942, car number 49's throttle was sticking, the brakes were bad and the steering too loose. Car 116 broke down on 22 March due to a petrol blockage and had to be towed from Newport Pagnell. There is no mention of the arrangement for an alternative method of transport for the passengers.

On 8 May 1942, a driver reported that the lights in car 91 'shine into the sky like a searchlight', rather than illuminate the road and refused to take out the vehicle again until the lights had been fixed. Another driver took out the vehicle on the same day and reported it unfit for the road. The driver of vehicle 235 had a traumatising day on 11 July 1942 when a lack of sufficient illumination from its lights caused her to drive into a bank at Padbury, killing two cats. The car was not damaged, but was marked to be fitted with an additional headlamp at the earliest possible opportunity. On 19 July 1942, car 32 broke down suddenly on the Water Eaton Road, where the driver abandoned it. Again, the report doesn't mention what happened to the passengers. On 25 April, the left back door of vehicle 598 continually flew open. The driver reported that several passengers had a narrow escape.

Not all recorded incidents were down to the condition of the vehicle. On 20 April 1943, J. Peters of the ATS was driving vehicle 508 along Church Green Road when a child ran out in front of her. The driver slammed on her brakes, but knocked the young girl onto the grass verge with a nudge of the bumper. The girl got up immediately and her mother 'said she was all right', so the driver carried on.

In the same week as Miss Nash's court hearing in October 1944, there were thirty-four working coaches trundling personnel around the local road network, with a further six on the blocks waiting for repair. The fleet also contained forty-five utility vehicles, thirty-one saloons, twenty-three vans, one military vehicle and one motorcycle, with twenty-five vehicles (inclusive of the six coaches) out of action. Some had private vehicles, but I believe the rules around these were strict because of fuel rationing, meaning that one could only drive in if the car carried a full contingent of passengers.

I distinctly remember travelling on a coach, much like the one shown on the Bletchley Park Roll of Honour entry for Gilbert Thomas Brown, the owner of the civilian transport contractor G.T. Brown Bus Company. At the outbreak of war, he was running a regular bus service between Stony Stratford and New Bradwell with four coaches, but his newest coach caught the attention of the War Office and was pressed into service picking up personnel billeted in the Stony Stratford, Wolverton and New Bradwell areas. His other three coaches followed suit and Mr Brown carried out his daily service until the end of the war. His coaches sound in a much better state of repair than the old, dilapidated coach I remember, which spluttered and rattled around the district in a slow endless circuit, but we made the best of it. It could be quite a hoot in the blackout with only the moon on a clear night to cast the face of your travelling companions out of the darkness. The content of the chatter was mostly irrelevant, but it was an opportunity to merrily chat to others outside of one's section, but we never discussed our work – ever.

According to the Roll of Honour entry for Gilbert Brown, the coach or utility vehicle stopped on arrival at the guarded gates because they were reportedly not allowed within the site. I seem to recall being dropped off inside the gate, but if it was outside the gate, it must have been a test of skill of the driver of the larger coaches to turn around in the restrictive confines of Wilton Avenue without crossing the boundary of the Park and evoking the ire of the guards, but I do remember that we had to show our Bletchley Park pass every time we entered. You did not dare forget it in fear of being refused entrance and the long arduous task of returning to your billet to collect it. If you lived too far away for that, you could ask someone from your office to collect you and confirm your identity with the guard. Either way, you walked into your office red-faced and in line for a reprimand for tardy and forgetful behaviour.

CHAPTER 16

JAPANESE MILITARY SECTION

By the time I joined the Japanese Military Section in about 1943, the work on Japanese codes at Bletchley Park was already underway. Brigadier Tiltman's Japanese Military Section, along with the most established of the Japanese sections – the Japanese Naval Section – and the newly formed Japanese Air Section each had offices off a central corridor, known as the 'Burma Road', in the newly constructed Block F.

In 1939, Brigadier Tiltman set to work on the Japanese naval code JN25 and broke it within a few weeks of starting the task. He went on to break the military attaché code in 1942 and the air force code the following year. Once the military attaché code was accessible, the Japanese Military Section was created in June 1942 to decipher the military attaché traffic, with material coming mainly from Foreign Office stations and Japanese communication from material received by air mail from India. Similar work was being carried out by other Japanese codebreaking sections in Washington, India, Australia and Canada.

At the end of March 1943, I returned from two weeks recovery from mumps in a reconditioning unit in Northampton. The journey there had been an adventure; we had to stop so I could be sick on the verge and I nearly fell over two officers on manoeuvres asking for a lift to Northampton. I said, if you want the mumps, you can have a lift but they declined the offer. I lost a stone in weight, which one of my male colleagues in the German Police Section said I needed to lose!

It was around this time that I moved to work in Hut 4 for Reginald Parker, a Foreign Office civilian working on German air and army codes for Hut 6. I was helping him get to grips with his paperwork, which was not easy, as he had a habit of scribbling over the entire page, then continuing round the edges in a spiral until every inch of paper was filled. It made my eyes go funny trying to untangle the words into a typed coherent report. I don't remember what I typed but it may have been related to Enigma because the Bletchley Park Roll of Honour shows he devised a system, 'Parkerismus', for revealing keys repeated by Enigma operators, giving codebreakers a way to break the key.

Before moving into Block F, the Military Section staff was still scattered in various locations, including the Mansion and Hut 5, which was positioned behind Hut 4. When the section moved into Block F in August 1943, all its sub-sections were amalgamated under a new 'Military Wing, GCHQ'.

Charles John William 'Don' Parkin was my boss in the Japanese Military Section in Block F, which included four offices of army and civilian personnel (ATS and Intelligence Corps staff) working twenty-four hours over three shifts. There were three ATS girls in my office and the change from working with men for three years went off without a hitch. Our office was terribly cramped; we had a desk each with a typewriter and the only other furniture I recall is some sort of filing cabinet that had to be locked at the end of each shift.

Don was in the office next to mine. He was 5 feet 10 inches with dark hair and kind brown eyes. He was a very kindly man, easy to get on with and this made working for him very pleasant, no doubt the reason why he was such a successful teacher before the war, well thought of and involved in lots of school activities. He was born in 1910 and worked as a school master at Christ's Hospital School in Horsham from 1932, gaining the rank of Second Lieutenant with the school's Training Corp. He volunteered for the ARP Casualty Service and kept the school's first aid training and provision up to date.

By the time he met and married Amy Rance, known by her middle name of Eileen in 1943, they were both at Bletchley. He may have started the six-month Japanese training course in Bedford soon after leaving the school and was on probation in Major Thompson's Japanese Section by the end of July 1943. Eileen would often call into the office for him, but I don't remember that she worked in our section.

He quickly proved his capabilities and in June 1944 was sent to Washington for the first official 'special mission' with the British Army Staff, which lasted until 23 June 1944. He became head of the sub-section at Bletchley from 1945, when he revisited Washington for a further two weeks in August 1945 and I remember meeting him on his visit to the Pentagon.

I also remember Sergeants Sandy Sanderson and Trixie Taylor; Captains John Brett-Smith and John Humphries and Lance Corporal Jimmy Bentley. I don't remember any of the other women in my office but I did become friends with Enid Noakes from the Japanese Section, but met her elsewhere and never knew she worked on Japanese until years later.

My service record does not help to substantiate the dates I moved to the Japanese Military Section, but it was about this time that more resources were pumped into reading Japanese codes. I also have a signed document dated 6 July 1944, which is almost a reiteration of the declaration I signed under the Official Secrets Act on my first day in 1941.

CERTIFICATE AND DECLARATION

1. *My attention has been drawn to the Extracts from the "Instructions for dealing with Documents and Correspondence in Military Offices, 934", set out in Appendix b to A.C.I. 609 of 1944, which relate to the safeguarding of military information.*
2. *I understand and agree that all official and military information acquired by me in the course of military duty, or any deductions which I may draw therefrom, is to be regarded as the property of the War Department, and is not to be published or communicated, either directly or indirectly, to another person in any form except in the course of my official duties, whether during or after I have left the Service, without the previous consent of the Army Council. I further understand that this undertaking is binding after the cessation of hostilities.*
3. *I further understand and agree that any breach or neglect of the above-mentioned Instructions for dealing with Documents and Correspondence in Military Offices, both as regards the safeguarding of official information and otherwise, is a disciplinary offence and may also render me liable to proceedings under the Official Secrets Acts, 1911 to 1939.*

I may also have signed this upon changing sections within the Government Code and Cypher School establishment, which would put the date I moved to the Japanese Section later than I thought. It has been suggested we were all required to sign after the UK and US signed an agreement to share intelligence. The document is a single page, whereas the Official Secrets Act was a stack, but its binding hold on me was no less significant. It is certainly similar to the one I signed when I went to Washington in 1945.

My duties in the Japanese Section included paraphrasing translated Japanese messages. It was considered a precaution to paraphrase messages we had picked up and decoded, so that if the Japanese intercepted one of our decoded messages passing on details of impending enemy troop movements in Burma and the impending counter-attack, the Japanese could not be certain we had broken their codes.

The paraphrased messages were sent in an inner and outer envelope, each with a coded address. I believe they were taken to a destination by despatch riders, but I did not know to whom.

Examples of translated messages with paraphrased version
Translated intercepted message
The target is to be the Capital on October 11 after dark.

Expect Kohima to be attacked 3 days from now by battalion strength.

Road from Meiktila to Kohima to be out of use for 4 days due to tanks assembling.

Expect attack early May, to west, probably Jap division 10.

Paraphrased version of message
London will be the target for night bombing on Tuesday 11 October.

Troops of 3rd Battalion will be moved to attack Kohima in 3 days' time.

The road between Meiktila and Kohima will be blocked on Monday to Thursday by tanks.

Division stationed Meiktila will attack from East – Mon May 1st.

Julia enjoyed her time in Air Section at first, but as the war progressed and work began to slow, the work became duller. She felt relieved when she transferred from the German Air Section to the Japanese Air Section.

In due course, I was what was known as 'enwised', which meant I went through the 'Entry Prohibited' door and was told that the main German code had been broken. It wasn't until about 1974 when the first books about Bletchley Park were published that I realised that this was Enigma, which I had never heard of hitherto! Life was now much more interesting. I had left my typewriter behind and found myself involved with the Enigma messages from which we were able to build up a complete picture of the Order of Battle of the German Luftwaffe Bomber Command and even know from which unit a Focke Wulf 200 aircraft had shot down the film star Leslie Howard in the Bay of Biscay. It was thought that the Germans imagined Churchill was to be on that particular plane and were trying to shoot him down.

This work continued until the end of the war in Europe. There were odd excitements, like finding myself on Operational Watch, which collected what one might call 'hot' information from various parts of the Air Section that were then reported immediately to Fighter Command at Stanmore. This information covered topics such as whether there was to be an air raid that night and, if so, where or whether E-boats were reported in the English Channel. All rather terrifying if one were left alone when the Watch Keeper, who normally dealt with this, went off for his supper and some query came through from Stanmore to which the chances were one didn't know the answer and had to stall madly knowing that it could be a matter of life or death and praying for the Watch Keeper to return quickly.

For the last few months in the German Air Section we had virtually nothing to do, as the Luftwaffe had either given up or had been sent to the Russian front. This was extremely tedious and to pass the time, I taught myself to write with my left hand, which I can still do! None of our work had the glamour and excitement of those deciphering Enigma etc. But it was of immense importance and is probably all filed away for posterity in some dark government dungeon!

Julia did not have the same enthusiasm for Japanese Air Section, as she was now tasked with recording older information on index cards.

This is almost a reversal of my experience, in which I enjoyed getting my teeth into more 'meaty' work within the Japanese Military Section and found paraphrasing messages more fulfilling than registering snippets of information on index cards, although I appreciate how crucial to the process my registration task was, even if it was painfully dull. Julia had swapped her interesting work on the operational watch for the painfully dull indexing.

I first revisited my work in the Japanese Section when Michael Smith contacted me for information for his excellent book *The Emperor's Codes* detailing the full history of the Japanese codebreaking at the Government Code and Cypher School.

Granny Brown holding my sister Margaret and me in the garden at Ryecroft, 1920s.

Betty taking in the view from the front garden at Ryecroft, mid-1930s.

Outside Mr & Mrs Paul's flat in Herrnhut, Germany, 1937.

With Elisabeth Paul outside her flat in Herrnhut, Germany, during my three-month stay with her family in 1937.

In Weston-super-Mare in the 1930s with my father, Leslie Vine-Stevens, and Margaret, my sister.

With my first boyfriend Otto Stoetzer, Summer 1938.

Under the wild cherry tree in the garden of Ryecroft with my mother and sister, Margaret.

Sitting beneath the cherry tree in the garden of Ryecroft – my bedroom window is visible in the background.

Me in 1941.

With Barbara Brown outside our billet at Salisbury House, Loughton, April 1943.

A telegram I sent to my father from Bletchley, circa 1942-45.

My friend Helen Little (née Colebrook), who served in the ATS within No. 6 Intelligence Service at Bletchley Park.

In uniform at the end of the war, 1945.

Walking down the street with
my colleague, John Burrows, in
Washington, DC, 1945. We worked
together in Bletchley Park's Japanese
Military Section before our posting
to the U.S.

A new and expensive hair-do before
leaving for Washington, DC, 1945.

Out shopping in Washington, DC,
1945.

Margaret Julia Mary Lydekker,
known as Julia, worked at Bletchley
Park from 1940 and served in
Washington, DC, from 1945 where
we met and became friends.

August 22nd 1945.

My darling Mummy.

Dorothea tells me you are still same! That's good cos I'm beginning to wonder whether I still am — there seems to be so much doing, + so much to think about before coming home. I simply must see some more of the country + buy as much as possible. However, although everything seems on top of me at the moment + I don't suppose it will be so bad when it comes to the point.

I'm sending this over by a friend who is returning, so you should have it by the week-end.

The weather is lovely now, still fairly hot,

but nothing like it was a month or so ago. Aunt Lois hasn't answered yet, but post is bad, so no doubt I'll have to wait a bit.

On Monday (20th Aug) I sent off the parcel with a surplice + sundry oddments. I have no idea how long it is likely to take but do tell me when it arrives.

Things which were rationed + hard to get over here during the war, are already coming back. So I hope in time to get fountain pens + all the other things we are in need of. It is really amazing - about 2 hours after the Jap surrender, petrol could be bought ad lib. And most groceries off points. I shouldn't think there's much hope of seeing the end of rationing at home yet, is there? Dorothea seems to have had a good holiday.

Oh, dear, I shall be so glad to get back Ma. There is so much indefinite news about demobbing, that I don't feel very enthusiastic about work. Still I'm almost certain to be in England by Xmas if not demobbed. So I mustn't grumble. Actually I'm still enjoying myself + there's plenty of interest to do.

This note paper + 'office'. + I don't suppose I should use it! So don't take any notice of the address at the top.

On reading this through I think it reflects my momentary bored + unsettled state. Sorry - hope the next one won't be so.

Much love to you all
Your loving Betts.

A letter I wrote to my mother on 22 August 1945 from Washington, DC.

Studying at secretarial college in
London, 1947.

With my father and mother, 1947.

In the garden at Ryecroft with my
mother and Jet, circa 1950s.

Sitting in the back garden at
Ryecroft with my mother and our
Agapanthus plants.

On stage (seated on right-hand side) with the Deeside Orpheus Music Society for the production of 'The Desert Song', October 1954.

I reverted to rank of Lieutenant in January 1961 to take up an administrative post at 71 (Bristol) Coy so I could be closer to my father in Herefordshire.

Around the time I retired from the WRAC in 1969.

With my husband Alfred Webb on our wedding day, 18 July 1970.

My wedding day with (left to right) Anne, my father's second wife; my father; Alfred; me; Jane Holley, my niece as flower girl; best-man Claude Jenks; and my sister, Margaret, 18 July 1970.

At the May 1994 opening of Bletchley Park Museum and inauguration of the Colossus Rebuild Project with Donald Foxley, son of Mr & Mrs Foxley, who I was billeted with in Loughton, during the war.

Beneath my named brick on the Codebreakers' Wall at Bletchley Park.

At Buckingham Palace after receiving my MBE, November 2015.

CHAPTER 17

BOMBS

I arrived at BP in October 1940 after a bomb had blasted out a wall of Hut 4. Bletchley wasn't the target, but became the victim of a bomber jettisoning its load over Bletchley on its way over the English Channel. As a rural area away from strategic military targets, my home in Richard's Castle also escaped the devastation rained down on the cities and coastal towns of Great Britain where the impact of the blasts sent tremors through every community. We could see the bombs in Birmingham as flashes of light over the Clee Hill and knew what it meant and could only feel for those who lived through it. Although Bletchley was not actively bombed, there was always a risk when travelling from London to Bletchley or home, as discovered by Margaret Rock, who wrote a letter home to her mother about being caught in a bombing raid while trying to get back to Bletchley in September 1940.

I got to Euston by 8.15 – the raids had just started and there were guns beginning, which soon got much louder. There was no train before my 9.50, so I asked a porter where I should wait. He directed me to an archway, a very long one going between the tube station and one of the platforms. The passengers and railway staff (in tin hats) spent all their time there, and it felt very safe, and never shook, however near the bombs. I sat there for some time, and talked to an Irish girl, just landed in England. She is coming to stay with and help her sister, who is expecting a baby, and lives in Wallington in Surrey. She was completely bewildered; she had sent her sister a time some days before and hoped someone would be there to meet her. But I expect the time hadn't been received yet. I told her to wait in the station or a shelter all night, and go on by herself in the morning. She has been here several times before and said, without my asking her, what a difference she had noticed in English people – how sociable they are now. She thought it a great improvement. All the time a tremendous noise was going on, but no one took much notice of it, nor did we. A friendly porter came and told us to come with him if we'd like to see a fire, and from the entrance of the archway there was the whole sky lit up flaming red. It was quite near either St Pancras or Kings Cross Station. Meanwhile, though we didn't know it, a very heavy bomb had dropped on the railway, just past the first signal boxes and all the trains had been delayed for hours while the railwaymen repaired the damage, which they did, although the inferno was going on all the time.

At 9.45 I went and sat in my train (everything was pitch dark, only lit by the continual flashes and a few dim lamps). A Scotch porter came and sat in the carriage with me and talked till we were told by the loud speaker that there was a delay, we could go back to the shelter. His company was very comforting, it felt lonely and unprotected on the train. He had been one of the volunteers the previous evening and had walked up and down each line to look for unexploded bombs. I went back to the Irish girl and a porter got us some tea from the free railway canteen. At 11 o'clock a cry went round – all passengers leave the station. We didn't know where to go, but had the way to the nearest shelter described to us, and at last found it, in Euston

Square. It was a now deathly quiet moment, luckily, only gunfire nearby, not bombs.

At 11.30 a railway man came and said the trains were running again, we could go back to the station. I took another farewell of the Irish girl and told her to stay where she was and try to sleep till the morning. I didn't like leaving her there alone, but I expect someone looked after her. Then again the handful of passengers got back to the station in the dark, I wishing I had a tin hat (and so did everyone else I expect). I was almost the only one for my train, and when I came to it I saw an air force man leaning out of a window so I joined him. I thought any company would be preferable to being alone on a night like that. The train didn't leave till after 2 o'clock so I was waiting in it 2½ hours, all very alarming, as the glass roof didn't feel like any protection at all!

The air force man and I talked all the time, I had a synopsis of his life, which I could repeat if there were time and space now. He told me, to reassure me, that he was married! (It was pitch dark, as we had to have the blinds down, so I didn't know what he looked like, except for the lighting of a cigarette.) The bombs sometimes fell very near, the man said 100 yards or so away, he thought they were still trying to get the station. Sometimes the German planes would come lower and lower overhead, one would hear its drone over everything. The train shook sometimes; really by the time we left I felt quite glad to be alive, though of course the railwaymen go through that every night. At last, at about 2.15, we left, and could go slowly over the damaged line.

There were a few 'near misses' later in the war, particularly in London. It was a time when the fear of V1 rockets clutched at your stomach every time you went to the city. As soon as the engine cut out you knew you were in trouble because that is when they dropped from the sky.

I remember arriving at Euston Station in a hiss of smoke and screeching brakes eager for a shopping trip in London. To my surprise, I stepped down onto the platform to find everyone drop to the floor. Without a thought I followed suit. I knew there was danger in the sudden silence. It was only when the air was punctured with the blast of the bomb hitting the ground nearby that I fully appreciated the dangerous moment I had arrived in.

The only other occasion was a time I had been sent for a two-week rest in a rehabilitation centre in Surrey in 1944. I had just arrived and was in the room unpacking my things when the sirens went off and I had to dive under the bed. It was a false alarm, but it was always a reminder that the threat of them was both terrifying and part of everyday life at the same time. One just had to get on with it and I find it hard to understand how on earth we adapted. My experiences were minor and ended well, and it is easy for me to say 'we adapted' as someone who never experienced first-hand the explosions, the searing flames, the crush of falling masonry and the wail of grief while digging in the rubble for loved ones. For that reason, one particular story has stayed with me all these years.

Sergeant Marcus Reginald Glover, who we called Mark, worked in the Japanese Military Section. He was also part of the BP drama club, enjoying fun and merriment as the assistant stage manager for one of the productions. Before the war he worked in banking and married Elsie Kilbey in 1929. They lived at 6 Carlton Street in East Barnet with their son Derek and Elsie's father, Henry

Kilbey, a retired music professor. It was a musical family with Elsie's brother a well-known musician playing in a trio with Max Jaffa and Jack Byfield. While Mark was serving at Bletchley, Elsie volunteered to the Women's Voluntary Service and the British Red Cross Service.

During the morning of 20 January 1945, the sky lit up with the explosion of a V2 rocket hitting East Barnet and another later that afternoon in Potters Bar. Unable to get hold of any news about his family, Mark was given leave to return home to check on them. When he arrived home, he found his house along with the entire street had been flattened by a direct hit.

Allan Rolfe in nearby Netherlands Road remembers the door blasted down the hallway narrowly missing his wife. Leslie Gregory of 11 Carlton Street was walking down the street when the rocket hit and was killed when the blast collapsed his lungs. His wife and daughter survived because they fell into the cellar as the house collapsed.

Two heavy-rescue units and a light unit with doctors, nurses and ambulances were helped by eleven heavy-rescue teams from other districts, with relief support from another eighteen rescue parties, all helping to locate and dig up casualties with the help of trained dogs. Allan Rolfe remembered digging out a man who was buried up to his neck.

The local Women's Voluntary Service managed an inquiry point, serving up cups of tea and feeding the helpers. On another day anywhere else in the district, Mark's wife Elsie would have been with them.

Allan Rolfe was later called upon to identify the bodies as a member of the East Barnet Civil Defence in charge of the household register. He doesn't list the names of those he found but Elsie and her father were killed, along with eight-year-old Derek. I will never forget the look on Mark's face after he returned to work. He quietly told us, 'All they found of my son was his tie.' That moment will stay with me for the rest of my life.

CHAPTER 18

SHENLEY ROAD MILITARY CAMP

After a year or so enjoying a billet with good food and my own room, it was a bit of a wrench to move into the Shenley Road Military Camp where each of the huts held more than thirty beds rather than the eighteen they were designed to accommodate. To make the best of it, we arranged our beds in a head-and-toe configuration down either side of the room and got out of bed in rotation to give us more room to dress. We each had a shelf and a barrack box on the floor at the foot of our bed for personal belongings.

The Shenley Road camp was built north of Bletchley Park, enabling the Government Code and Cypher School to free up billets in the surrounding towns and villages for civilians and merge military personnel near the park. Thirty-two women in the ATS moved into the camp towards the end of May 1942, with numbers only peaking at 350 in August 1944. Both men and women in the army moved into the camp, with eight men moving in at the beginning of January 1944 and reaching 392 men at the camp by the end of August.

The mattress was three square stuffed mattresses, known as palliasses, which would slip and slither through the night and became wedged into the gaps of the bed frame. We sacrificed one of our three blankets to parcel the palliasses together and create one serviceable mattress from three hopeless ones. Jimmy Thirsk was told to collect his three palliasses from the Quartermaster's store and fill them with straw. Anyone with previous experience stuffed them until the stitching stretched so they didn't become flattened into pancakes. Straw, after a comfortable bed and my own room at Salisbury House! I feel fortunate to have vanquished all but a single memory of those mattresses!

The huts were built from breeze blocks with no insulation or ventilation and were freezing in winter and boiling in summer. Each hut had two coke stoves fuelled by wood and coke. They were very difficult to fire and caused horrid clouds of smoke, despite a chimney designed to carry the smoke up through the roof into the air above. The chimneys were unprotected, and the heat of the bare metal could melt your skin if touched. For the most part, we left it unlit and when it was cold enough to freeze our flannels, we charged around for a hectic game of table tennis in the mess just before bedtime then rushed under the covers while our circulation was at its best.

We had to keep our bunks spotless and make our beds in a specific way. Every Monday we had to polish an allocated section of floor in the barracks with a sort of bitumen-type polish until it shined. It was a horrid job. I don't recall other chores, but I've read of another ATS recruit despairing at the scenes she faced on latrine duty.

The separate ablution block comprised a row of wash basins and several baths, but not enough for all of us. The worst part was sitting on the cold floor waiting for your turn. By the time it came around, five inches of hot water and a wooden duck board to stand on to save you from stepping out of the bath onto the cold floor with bare feet were insufficient to drive out the chill in your bones or make you feel refreshed.

Apart from table tennis – my favourite game – Shenley Road also had darts. There was even a bar, but very rarely anything to drink. The camp had a perimeter fence, but in the hot summer we would take our bedding into a nearby field to cool down. Once or twice, we even slept there and made a hasty retreat back to our huts in the morning. We never got caught, but then our hut was the last hut nearest the field.

The women's and men's sleeping quarters were separate, but food was served in the mess so we all ate together. Mother came to visit towards the end of the war and I was able to take her to lunch in the mess. I am sure the food wasn't anywhere as near as good as the meal she would have received had she visited while I was billeted with the Foxleys. Now she could experience a bit of my life at Bletchley Park for the first time. It was a chance to see the town and witness me in my uniform surrounded by the hustle and bustle of the camp.

Our camp came under the severe military command of Lieutenant Colonel Fillingham of the Durham Light Infantry. It boiled his blood that he was not allowed into Bletchley Park and he could not understand why he was not privy to the goings-on within the perimeter. He barked orders as if it was a regular military camp, without regard for the unique set-up. On one occasion, he had the stones laid around some of the huts painted white. In the circumstances, it seemed an unnecessary use of paint and time. I've read elsewhere that this might have been for a VIP visit, but I don't recall one. I'm sure we would have been suited and booted, with every button shining. He liked to find ways of asserting control and did this through his regular demands for proper military behaviour, making sure that any of the men in Military Section who had joined as civilians and been absorbed into the army without the experience of basic training were properly introduced to the drills, saluting, marching and other features of the hierarchy of army life.

CHAPTER 19

SECURITY BREACHES

The campaign for silence started early in the war and I remember the posters with phrases such as Be like Dad, Keep Mum; Careless Talk Cost Lives and The Walls Have Ears emblazoned in large letters and accompanied by amusing cartoons to make them memorable. The ATS used the Soldier's Service and Paybook as a method of reminding us of the importance of discretion. Every time I opened it, I was faced with a security reminder at the beginning of the book.

ALL RANKS. Remember – Never discuss military, naval or air matters in public or with any stranger, no matter to what nationality he or she may belong. The enemy wants information about you, your unit, your destination. He will do his utmost to discover it. Keep him in the dark. Gossip on military subjects is highly dangerous to the country, whereas secrecy leads to success. BE ON YOUR GUARD and report any suspicious individual.

The army required us to carry this book with us at all times. It was our identity pass and contained a space to record every training course, posting, inoculation and medical rehabilitation, and also our reminder to keep mum. These were reminders, whereas the Official Secrets

Act document I signed on my first day at Bletchley Park was law, and if I had ever been in doubt about the need for utter discretion, that ended when I signed my name on that document and I took the responsibility of it to heart.

Bletchley had its own unofficial 'secrecy' form to remind staff of the dangers of careless talk. It was a single sheet setting out a list of places to be mindful of talking.

SECRECY

This may seem a simple matter. It should be. But repeated experience has proved that it is not. Even for the cleverest of us; even for the least important. Month after month, instances have occurred where workers at BP have been heard casually saying outside BP things that are dangerous.

It is not enough to know that you must not hint at these things outside. It must be uppermost in our mind every hour that you talk to outsiders. Even the most trivial-seeming things matter. The enemy does not get his intelligence by great scoops, but from a whisper here, a tiny detail there. Therefore:

DO NOT TALK AT MEALS. There are waitresses and others who may not be in the know regarding your own particular work.

DO NOT TALK IN THE TRANSPORT. There are drivers who should not be in the know.

DO NOT TALK TRAVELLING. Indiscretions have been overheard on Bletchley platform. They do not grow less serious further off.

DO NOT TALK IN YOUR BILLET. Why expect your hosts, who are not pledged to secrecy, to be more discreet than you, who are?

DO NOT TALK BY YOUR OWN FIRESIDE, whether here or on leave. If you are indiscreet and tell your own family, they may see no reason why they should not do likewise. They are not in a position to know the consequences and have received no guidance. Moreover, if one day invasion came, as it perfectly well may, Nazi brutality might stop at nothing to wring from those that you care for, secrets that you would give anything, then, to have saved them from knowing. Their only safety will lie in utter ignorance of your work.

BE CAREFUL, EVEN IN YOUR HUT. *Cleaners and maintenance staff have ears, and are human.*

The form has another section warning that too many people already know that something hush-hush is going on at Bletchley Park. It ends with the declaration, 'I hereby promise that no word of mine shall betray, however slightly, the great trust placed in me' and a space for the reader to sign their name.

With so many reminders about the dangers of careless talk and the need for secrecy, as well as the burden of the Official Secrets Act, I had thought instances of indiscretion were rare, which is how I answer when someone asks at one of my talks if the secrecy was breached. It has since been disappointing to learn of so many incidents to the contrary. At my talks, I have shared examples ranging from minor indiscretions to more serious transgressions, often involving a bit of showing off or fishing for information out of curiosity rather than mischief, and the odd occasion of a stray secret document.

The security breaches file in the National Archive records interesting examples of the sort of security risks of which I have included a few below. One such breach occurred in the March/April 1944 edition of a school magazine in which a birth announcement says one former pupil is now serving with the Wireless Experimental

Depot, India Command. It goes on to describe the wife's accomplishments as 'taking military education classes and also helping her husband in translating wireless messages, being a Japanese linguist, among other accomplishments'.

Bletchley Park Deputy Director Nigel de Grey's comments that, 'We have always been warned of the danger of Parish and School Magazines' suggests such sources were rife with indiscretion and, while the breach occurred abroad, the work mentioned is directly related to Bletchley Park and could have had serious consequences if read by the wrong person. Compartmentalisation was used as an extra layer of security, so only a select few had an understanding of the overall operation. Each person should only know about their immediate duties and was not permitted to enter into other huts or buildings or even other offices within their department without permission.

In August 1943, Max Newman, head of the Newmanry, was asked to reprimand one of his staff for entering Hut 11A, which housed the bombe machines, without written permission

It was easy to get caught out with a slip of the tongue; on 19 April 1944 it was reported that a civilian working in Hut 6, Block D, had fallen foul of the rules by informing 'her billetor and several other people at Wolverton that a knowledge of German is required for the work here'.

The security breach file contains incidences of a number of verbal indiscretions to American service officers. Most incidents were investigated and resolved with a stern warning, but occasionally the attitude of the transgressor required other action, as in the case of a Wren working on Special Duties X (SDX) at one of the outstations. When challenged, the Wren denied giving any information to an American officer, despite being presented with statements from several witnesses. Nigel de Grey took a harsh view after he could get no further with her, 'except a stolid denial' of passing on information.

She seemed quite incapable of grasping that the matter had any importance. Her apparent attitude was one of complete indifference to the whole thing. I was not well impressed with her mentality or character, both of which struck me as of a decidedly lower standard than I have been accustomed to finding among the SDX WRNS to whom I have spoken.

Under the circumstances I consider that she should be employed on other duties of a non-confidential character and that the risk of allowing her to go elsewhere would be smaller than her continued presence in Secret work, especially as she appeared quite unmoved at any such prospect.

I think she should be watched by her officers and any deterioration reported immediately to NID [Naval Intelligence Division]. Her general behaviour will probably afford a useful guide to her security.

The rules on sharing information internally were no less strict, as two Foreign Office civilians found following a breach of security arising out of laziness.

On the morning of 23 June 1945, a Miss G. from Naval Section handed in her friend's wallet, a Miss P. in Naval Section (Hut 18, Japanese language school), after a night out at a hop in the Assembly Rooms. The security office quizzed Miss P when she called into the security office to collect it an hour later. She admitted to loaning the wallet, so that her friend could use her BP pass to go to supper in the canteen rather than collect her own pass from her quarters in the women's hostel. Miss P said she 'did not think there was any harm in it as I knew her so well'. With Miss P off on weekend leave after the hop, the two women arranged a handover in the security office because they considered it the safest place. The security report for the incident finishes with, 'As you know there have been other similar cases of this sort and you may wish to take drastic action to prevent the practice continuing.' The report does not say if the women were given a telling off or a more severe punishment, as was recommended, but both girls may have wished Miss G had just opted to collect her pass from the hostel, which was only a short walk away from the cafeteria.

There were so many ways to slip up when it came to security and one had to be on guard at all times. With the image of the revolver looming somewhere in the back of mind, I buttoned up and said nothing about my work and only shared where I lived once it was acceptable to do so. After the war, I put the entire time out of my head and over the years the memories were buried, so when we were able to talk about our time at Bletchley Park, it was hard to remember many details. In the mid-1970s, I worked in an office in Birmingham and frequently crossed paths in the streets nearby with a woman whom I recognised from Bletchley. I didn't know her name, but we would acknowledge one another with a nod of greeting and understanding. A little later, after Fred Winterbotham's book was published about codebreaking during the war, *The Ultra Secret*, the woman called across the street to me. 'It's out,' she said, and I replied, 'What's out?' 'We can talk,' she called back, and I thought, I don't want to.

It is with lasting regret that I never had the chance to tell my parents about my experiences during the war and it wasn't something I thought of telling my sister. With the age difference and such different personalities, we were not close, but I will never forget the time she was at a talk I gave years later and I couldn't remember the post office box number for Bletchley. She had the number on the tip of her tongue. It made me realise, she had learnt about and was interested in my wartime years.

CHAPTER 20

SERVICE ABROAD

It was 9 May 1945, the war in Europe was won. Stewart Menzies, the Chief of the Government Code and Cypher School and the intelligence service wasted no time in sending out a message.

On this ever memorable day, I desire that all who are doing duty in this Organisation should be made aware of my unbounded admiration for the way in which they had carried out their allotted tasks.

Such have been the difficulties, such has been the endeavour and such have been the constant triumphs that one senses that words of gratitude from one individual are perhaps out of place. The personal knowledge of the contribution made towards winning the War is surely the real measure of the thanks which so rightly belong to one and all in a great and inspired organisation which I have the privilege to direct. This is your finest hour.

Many people began to return to their lives and families, but the conflict was not yet over for some of us. The war with Japan was still in progress and our attention moved towards redistributing some staff within Bletchley Park to postings abroad. I volunteered for work abroad at the beginning of March 1945 for 'service in India or Ceylon'.

Women in the ATS could only serve abroad if they had volunteered and only upon production of a letter of permission from their parents. Only one in thirty parents gave permission by the end of 1944, so the government stepped in to free up the female workforce with legislation, which came into force in February 1945. It did not go down well with anxious parents who wanted to keep their daughters safe on home soil. There was only a month between the change in the law and the date I completed the form. Although I did not need my parents' permission, I am sure they would have signed the letter had I volunteered a month earlier. I had signed a declaration to say 'I could be ordered to proceed at short notice' and was 'liable to be despatched to any overseas station to which ATS are posted, without reference to my individual preference of station' for at least two years.

Every day, I walked the well-trodden path between my billet in the camp and the gate into Bletchley Park, always stopping off at the Company Office along the way. The Company Office was an army administration office within the military camp and we were expected to keep up to date with orders posted on its noticeboard.

One day I scanned the noticeboard and found my name on a list of staff earmarked for deployment to Delhi. I still have a copy of my application to serve abroad, which shows it took two months for the Commanding Officer of the ATS Shenley Road Camp and Commanding Officer 1 Coy, ATS to each authorise my request, so the notice must have been posted at the end of April or beginning of May 1945.

I reported to Company Office soon after for an interview to assess my suitability for Delhi. I don't remember the interview other than that there were about twenty of us volunteers, but I imagine the decision about whom to deploy had already been made. The interview covered travel instructions and a stern warning that as ambassadors of HM Forces we should behave appropriately.

I somehow knew I would not be going to Delhi. It's hard to describe other than as a strange premonition, which was not uncommon in my life. I was so sure I was not going that I have never given a thought to how different my experience would have been had I served in India. The next day Don Parkin, head of the Japanese Section, called me to his office and told me I would not be going to India after all. It was still surprising news, despite my inkling, because I had signed the form, a copy of which is in the service record I obtained from the Ministry of Defence, to say that 'once nominated to proceed on embarkation leave, draft, or with a unit overseas I may only withdraw my name on the most urgent compassionate grounds and must submit my application in writing for the approval of the appropriate authority.'

I soon realised my overseas adventure was not cancelled, but modified; I was going to Washington. In fact, I would be working in the newly constructed Pentagon building. Exciting, I thought, even though I knew little of it at that time. I felt honoured to be chosen, especially as I was the only member of the ATS to be posted there – a humble staff sergeant!

All would become clear, but before heading across the ocean I had to complete a very important mission – to the hairdresser. In those days, it wasn't a simple operation and I had to travel to Oxford for an appointment at an upmarket hairdresser managed by two Cypriot men. It was worth the time and the expensive four guineas price tag for a perm that lasted throughout my time in the humid conditions of America. With a new hairstyle, I was ready for anything.

After a short embarkation leave, I travelled to Euston Station on 12 May 1945, then to the War Office Holding Unit, ATS, 12 Radnor Place, London, located near Hyde Park. The unit was a holding camp for army staff waiting for deployment outside the country and I was on my way to collect my movement orders with travel instructions. I arrived to find there was a problem with my papers and I was obliged to remain at the holding centre until it could be resolved. I was supposed to be escorting a member of the West Indian ATS, Therese de Freitas, from Jamaica to Washington, where she was due to meet her mother at our hotel.

The number of women from the West Indies who served is some 300 serving in the Caribbean and 100 serving in Great Britain. The War Office had resisted the Colonial Office's proposal to allow West Indian women to enlist in the ATS, but some Black women did join up and were already serving in the Caribbean although, as a copy of the West India Committee Circular shows, Trinidadian Private Ivy Belboda had been studying at a London university when war broke out and subsequently enlisted in the ATS. She appears on the May 1942 list and is photographed with Lieutenant Colonel Sir Ivan Davson, the chairman of the West Indian Committee, at an anti-aircraft site in Cardiff, where she worked as a radio locations operator. Each month, the Committee Circular listed those who served. The WAAF had accepted a handful of Black women into its ranks following the RAF's lift of a 'colour ban' in 1940. There is no mention of Miss de Freitas, but the list relies on members of the committee submitting names for publication so may not be complete.

It took two years, but the tug of war on the recruitment of Black West Indian women into the ATS was won when the extra hands necessary to meet the needs of an overstretched army fighting on multiple fronts heaved the outcome of the decision onto the side of the Colonial Office. ATS Director Jean Knox also pushed for the new West Indian recruits to work in Washington, but the War Office insisted that only white West Indian women could serve in the US, despite the Colonial Office's objection to the ban. Thus it was that 200 white West Indian women served in the US and Black West Indian recruits began to arrive in Great Britain in October 1943.

With no resolution to my travel papers problem, Miss de Freitas continued on alone to meet the ship and sail to Washington without me. I believe that Miss de Freitas was travelling home to Jamaica after meeting her mother in Washington, but I have not been able to find out more about her or her journey to Washington. I, meanwhile, had no option but to wait at the holding centre, sleeping in basic accommodation while I waited for further instructions.

The Whitsun holiday at the end of May 1945 was the first holiday since the outbreak of war that people were able to visit London without fear of bombings. It was no holiday for me, however, because I had been waiting in the holding centre since 12 May waiting for my papers, which lay unopened on the desk of the officer responsible for my movement order, who was on leave. My service record shows I was going to be posted away from the holding centre on 21 May 1945, but the order was cancelled, and I remained waiting for news of my travel, anxious that my posting in Washington would be cancelled and someone else would be chosen to go. There was no way I wanted the opportunity to pass me by, so I decided I could wait no longer and began to see if I could get things moving myself.

CHAPTER 21

WASHINGTON DC

Following a telephone call to the head of the Japanese Section, Don Parkin, to explain why I was still in London, he quickly arranged for me to be seen by another department in the War Office. The problem was soon resolved and someone sorted out the movement order. I had missed the ship and now there was an urgency to get me over to Washington. I was to travel via Poole and catch a flying boat to Baltimore, a means of travel usually reserved for private passengers and high-ranking officials. Until recently, I had thought it was a Sunderland flying boat, but the register of vessels arriving at and departing from Foynes shows it was a British Overseas Airways Corporation Boeing 314A called *Bangor*. The army didn't usually pay for small fry like me to fly.

Once I arrived at Poole, I boarded a small boat to cross the water from the harbour to the flying boat's mooring. I felt every dip and swell on the short boat ride from the harbour and began to be terribly sick, which was not helped by having to climb unceremoniously onto its wings to get on board.

This was my first flight and I was extremely scared to be taking to the skies in such uncertain times. Who knew what would be waiting for us up beyond the clouds? I was also unnerved by the anonymity of the civilian clothes worn by my fellow passengers. I was in uniform, but the other passengers were all male and wearing civilian clothes, which made me more nervous because I feared they might ask me what I was doing and where I was going. The image of the revolver on the desk at Bletchley Park was still vivid in my mind.

Fortunately, none of the men spoke to me. I must have been a most unattractive travelling companion, as I was quite unable to stop my sickness, even though the pilot kindly gave me some pills; they didn't help!

The first stop was Foynes in County Limerick, Ireland to refuel and eat. It was dark and I felt too ill to eat or enquire where we were. We climbed back aboard the Boeing 314A to find the seating had been rearranged so that we could lie down and sleep. We soon took off again and continued to fly due east for what seemed to be an endless sleepless night. Finally, we came down through a beautiful morning mist to land at Botwood, on the Canadian island of Newfoundland.

We looked out over a vast expanse of fir trees as we ate breakfast at the airport. I was amazed to see bacon and eggs on the menu and found it ignited my appetite. I happily ate the bacon and eggs as well as trying Grape-Nuts, which is a breakfast cereal that contains neither grapes nor nuts, but is made from wheat and barley. The breakfast worked wonders at easing my travel sickness and finally I was able to enjoy our flight southwest, over the United States of America to Baltimore.

Feeling weak and tired I was relieved to get out of the Boeing at last. Captain John Burrows from my section at Bletchley Park met me at the airport to escort me on the final leg of my journey to Washington DC. John was born Lionel Burrows in 1912, but went by his middle name.

He was a teacher of modern languages when war broke out in 1939 and was posted with the Intelligence Corps to manage intelligence for the commander in chief in Singapore. He was on duty in the naval base near Kanji the night the Japanese invaded. He was evacuated to Java before Singapore fell to the Japanese on 15 February 1942, and made his way to Bletchley Park. Thousands of other Allies were not so lucky and spent the rest of the war in Japanese prisoner-of-war camps. At Bletchley Park he led a Japanese traffic analysis section.

Years later I asked John why he had chosen me for Washington. He simply answered 'because I thought it was a good idea'. My friendship with John and his wife lasted for the remainder of his life.

I still have the Movement Order typed on the British Army Staff Movements Branch letterhead paper with the address 605 Garrett Building, Redwood and South Streets, Baltimore. It records my 'posting for duty to British Army Staff' taking a direct route from Baltimore by train on 1 June 1945 at 17:57, arriving at 18:40. I used the travel warrant to secure my seat and the taxi to transport us from the train station to my billet at the Cairo Hotel on 16th and Q streets. I was too tired to take in much as I waved John off with a thank you for his kindness.

Once again, this experience contrasts with that of Julia, whose journey to Washington via Halifax in Canada had all the elements of a disorganised disaster on the part of the Foreign Office, who failed to plan her trip adequately. As a civilian, she did not have her uniform as a calling card to indicate she was on official business and she had to rely on her own wit and luck for a large proportion of her journey. Describing her experience in her memoir, Julia said:

Early in 1945, I was informed I was being sent from the Japanese Section at Bletchley Park to work in the Pentagon in Washington DC for time unspecified, but presumably until the war ended. At that time there was no inkling whatever about atom bombs and one assumed the war would continue in the mainland of Japan until the Japanese were defeated – probably one to two years. This move naturally caused consternation to my parents who were horrified at the idea, but they took it with equanimity. It caused me to panic too – setting off into the unknown all by myself, as although others came and went to Washington, nobody was going at the same time as myself. However, my old friend Philip Howse, who had been billeted at the vicarage, was already there, so at least there was someone I knew. This was also somewhat of a relief to my parents as well. I didn't have very much notice and so packed my two suitcases with what I thought I might need and, clothes being strictly rationed at the time, I had to make do with what I had. I was sailing in May (the day after VE Day), so there was a need for winter things. Later, clothes in Washington were quite a revelation. Because of mass-produced clothes being in the only range I could afford, one was rather inclined to meet a replica of oneself walking down the street, which could be rather startling.

Julia's matching outfit experience reminds me of a similar occasion I had in which I was sitting on a train wearing a new and expensive tweed suit. I remember strutting to the train station feeling the bee's knees and settling down for the journey. Out of the corner of my eye, I caught a reflection of myself, but on closer inspection it wasn't a reflection at all, but another woman wearing the same suit in the same colour, taupe. The journey was uncomfortable from that point, because it took quite a lot of effort for each of us to feign nonchalance and avoid eye contact.

I was used to travelling alone by train from a young age, when my parents sent me and my sister by train to Weston-Super-Mare to see Granny. We each wore a label with words to the effect that we were Cecil Stockton's family and the guards looked after us. This was good training for my train journey to Germany without adult supervision in 1937. A trans-Atlantic trip could be said to be the next step, but I am sure my parents would have been more noticeably anxious had I travelled earlier in the war when there was a high risk of a German attack. With the cessation of the war in Europe, those risks had all but disappeared and my parents didn't express any concern about my next posting. Julia found her mother's anxiety was less easy to pacify.

I was to sail from Swansea, which was a dead secret of course from a security point of view, but my mother, father and friend Ann Lavell came to see me off from Paddington. At the very last moment, as the train was about to pull out of the station, Mother said she was coming too and climbed into the train, ticket-less and luggage-less, leaving behind on the platform two startled and singularly glum faces – both of whom were convinced they would never see me again.

On arrival at Swansea, the centre of which was no longer there after being bombed flat, we somehow found a taxi, which took us to some particularly seedy hotel where I had accommodation booked. It was very difficult at that period of the war and after so much bombing to find anywhere to stay. On arrival at the reception desk, some minion asked us if we were the cooks they were expecting. As we needed a room for the night, I quickly agreed that we were, imagining I would probably have to cook the breakfast. It wasn't until years afterward that I realised the travel agent that had arranged my passage and booked my hotel was Thomas Cook. Silly me.

We were too late for any food, so retired to a very scruffy single room with only one bed. With my mother still with me, we had to sleep head to toe, but by then we were really past any sleep and had an exhausting night in consequence. We had an animated conversation to the effect that our pillows were so awful that they were obviously filled with coal.

Come the morning and it was impossible to force down any breakfast – not my best time in any circumstances. We went by taxi to the Agent's office at the docks, where my papers were checked. I then went one way and my mother went the other way to catch a train back to London.

On 25 May 1945, Julia boarded the Cunard White Star *SS Tortuguero* with ten other passengers, including a family of four emigrating to Canada; the captain of a merchant ship on his way to collect his next vessel, who 'retired to his cabin with several crates of whisky and wasn't seen again until we arrived at the other end'; and a secretive chap in an expensive camel-hair coat, who Julia suspected of being a black-marketeer. According to the passenger manifest, he was an export sales manager for Smart & Brown (Engineers), and belonged to a family that included an Admiralty architect. Julia's descriptions of her fellow passengers make them sound like characters in a riveting Agatha Christie novel and no doubt they helped to ease her boredom during the voyage:

We set sail from Swansea, but got only as far as Milford Haven where we were joining a convoy. Much hanging around here, but eventually all were shepherded together and we set off on our adventure. After a day at sea a message from the British Admiralty arrived to say that the war was over in Europe and, as there were no more German U-boats around (we hoped), the convoy could disperse and everyone got off at their own speed. So everyone else disappeared at speed over the horizon, but SS Tortuguero *chugged along in the rear. It was, in fact, the very last convoy to assemble and then leave the United Kingdom in World War 2 and so was of historical interest.*

After about a day at sea we ran into a gale and the ship being in ballast caused it to jump about all over the place – pitch, toss and roll – so I retired to my bunk and reckoned that was that for the time being. However, the chief steward had other ideas and arrived in my cabin saying, 'Come along Miss, get dressed and come up on deck and I will bring you lunch.' Horrors! However, I made the effort and went up to where the kind chap had arranged a chair and rug for me and, having wrapped me up well, went off to get lunch. An enormous helping of pork with all the trimmings and vegetables arrived, enough meat to have been the ration for four of us for a week at home. It is funny how there are some meals that one remembers! I realised that in fact I was rather hungry and polished off nearly all of it, taking care to breathe in when the ship rose and out when it went down, as instructed by Mama who had actually done cross-channel and the Harwich to Hook run several times while studying in Germany.

About a week out from America we were told that we were going to Halifax, Nova Scotia, rather than New York, which was a bore because I wondered how to get from Halifax to New York, but all was resolved in due course.

I imagine my journey to the US would have been similar had I travelled by ship with Miss de Freitas, as originally intended, although reading Julia's description of the pitching ship is enough to bring back memories of my debilitating sickness on my short boat trip from dock to flying boat. I am relieved the army was more organised and I had Don Parkin at the end of the telephone to sort out alternative plans. Julia was not so fortunate:

We were now at last on Canadian soil and had our first glimpse of Canadian efficiency with regard to travel when we collected our tickets and 'checked through' our surplus luggage. This later meant that we had no trouble with chasing after guards' vans and porters (or 'red caps', as they were known in the New World). We merely checked baggage through to Washington and, on arrival, it would be there on the same train as us, having travelled all the way with us, but without the bother and fuss of looking after it. Travelling in an official capacity, I was pounced upon by two enormous, extremely fierce looking Canadian Mounted Policemen who, with unsmiling faces, came up and stood either side of me, having solemnly introduced themselves and asked if there was anything they could do. As I had quite expected by their general demeanour that an arrest was imminent, this was rather an anti-climax. However, a few questions showed that they obviously knew nothing about where I was supposed to go, which incidentally I didn't either, apart from the fact that I knew Washington was my goal. After a few minutes of somewhat fruitless questions, we parted the best of friends with much handshaking and hat-raising and so ended my first interview with the Law on this side of the Atlantic.

By the time I finally arrived in Washington, I realised that I had no idea where I was to go, having failed to ask before leaving Bletchley Park and not having been told by anyone there what I was to do in America except to work in the Pentagon. So this was a 'how do you do'! However, I reckoned that the British

Embassy was my best bet and having chummed myself up with a nice American colonel on the train who was apparently going past the Embassy, I was given a lift there by him in his yellow cab.

It being a Sunday the Embassy, which was a very grand and rather pretentious Lutyens building, was quite deserted except for a caretaker who rather grudgingly managed to contact a rather cross secretary, who arrived in due course announcing that they had wondered what had happened to me. Would they have bothered to find out, one wonders? I discovered later that various others coming over from the UK also got stuck in Canada and failed to appear when expected, so maybe it was the norm, although I believe there was some sort of system if one arrived in New York, as expected.

Eventually I was parked in a hotel, which was quite comfortable, but I was told very firmly by the receptionist that it was only a temporary stay for a week at the most and thereafter I should have to find my own accommodation.

I rang Philip Howse, who was unfortunately away for the weekend, but he rang me later and took me out to breakfast the next day. He was not working in the Pentagon, but someone arrived to take me there. I spent the next week getting lost, either in the Pentagon or in Washington.

Chapter 22

THE PENTAGON

In Washington to finally get some sleep before starting work the next day, I quickly found my room, which I was to share with Pip Wallace, another ATS girl, who came from Hull. I didn't know it then on that first night, or was too tired to care, but the hotel was very uncomfortable and did not have air-conditioning. The oppressive hundred-degree-heat, high humidity and constant battle with the thriving cockroaches in my room were the only drawbacks of my five-month stay in the capital city. Pip turned out to be a very good cockroach catcher, which was a good thing, since every night we had to kill as many as possible before we could go to bed wrapped in bath towels to combat the sticky heat.

The next morning I dressed in my uniform, quickly realising that I would perspire from the moment I did up the last button of my jacket until I stripped it all off again. Soon after my arrival, however, on 6 June, to my relief, I collected new kit – five khaki cotton shirts, three summer skirts, two summer ATS caps, two summer jackets and one waterproof coat. The shirts and skirts were a lighter Canadian Women's Army Corps issue, which were coupled with the British summer jacket when full uniform was required. I also picked up four pairs of rayon stockings and two pairs of lisle stockings. As soon

151

as I got the new kit back to the hotel, the skirts, shirts and stockings I had brought with me from England went back in the kit bag for the rest of my time in Washington. The stockings were treasure and I wore them when I returned home, to much jealousy. They felt so light compared to those issued at home, but I sweltered in serge for the first few days.

I travelled to the Pentagon for the first time on the bus like a wide-eyed sightseer during the twenty- to thirty-minute journey past the White House, over the Arlington Bridge and Potomac River into the state of Virginia. The Pentagon is in Arlington in Virginia, but has a postal address in Washington DC (District of Colombia). I experienced racial segregation for the first time during these bus journeys – white passengers at the front of the bus and Black passengers at the back.

From a distance, the Pentagon towered out of the landscape of open space and seemed to grow ever taller as the bus approached closer to the outer and largest pentagon. I don't imagine the view is as uninterrupted nowadays. Each of the five external sections span half a mile, with four further concentric pentagons and each one connected by a series of corridors spanning seventy and a half miles. According to the brochure I picked up while working in the building, the Pentagon was built to merge together the scattered staff of every department of the War Department beneath one roof and still have room to expand up to 40,000 people. The document reads like a promotional brochure, but it helped me navigate such an enormous space. I was relieved I did not have to rely on a brochure that first day; my dear friend John Burrows was once again there to meet me from the bus and escort me to a meeting with the section head.

The 32,000 workers who passed through the building over a twenty-four-hour period each day all entered the building via a vast, busy concourse lined with shops, a bank, a medical centre and a church. Security was tight and access to the concourse was only granted upon presentation of your pass to the US army personnel stationed at each access point. The same procedure was repeated outside your office. This happened every day without fail. I remember I was friendly with one of the American girls who checked the passes and one day I asked in frustration if she really needed to check my details. She still checked my details and did so every day that I worked in the building.

Colonel O'Connor was the American section head, whose staff included John Burrows, James Pope-Hennessey (later, Queen Mary's biographer), me and others from other US and UK services. I seem to recall that the majority of general staff were women and we worked in a large open-plan office accessed via a ramp from the main concourse.

I had a desk and typewriter, where I was tasked with paraphrasing intelligence reports derived from the intercepted Japanese communications from Burma. Although the four-year Burma campaign was effectively at an end by the time I arrived in Washington, the Japanese forces did not surrender until the end of August 1945. The process of paraphrasing was identical to my duties at Bletchley and although I don't remember exactly the contents, I do recall there was a constant flow of signals passing between Japanese forces, which kept me busy between my work hours of 9 am to 5 pm.

At the end of the day, we had to sign out and make our way back along the concourse to wait for the bus. During the first week, Julia had to return to her temporary billet but then had to sort out a more permanent billet arrangement. Once again, the army had been more organised and had arranged accommodation for the duration of my time. Julia relates:

Fortunately the Embassy had a rudimentary accommodation section, so I went off there to find a very nice motherly lady who had something that 'might do'. Eventually, I arrived at 2003 Kalorama Road after, as usual, being carried past it by the bus. I couldn't afford a taxi because they were very expensive and my money was very short, so I arrived somewhat late for my interview. This street was in a very select part of Washington and consisted of large, terrace houses. Number 2003 was officially known as a boarding house, but turned out to be much more of a ladies' club full of interesting people, although it was difficult to discover who was actually in residence or had just dropped by. My landlady was a delightful person. She was a Professor at Charlottesville University and was currently working in the OSS (Office of Strategic Studies, which was the precursor of the CIA) and was an authority on the Balkans. She had also worked in the British Museum and, to my surprise, I discovered that she knew well a family living in Leighton Buzzard with whose daughter I had been at preparatory school, so that was a good introduction.

Julia had found accommodation she liked and a landlady she could get on with, but the downside was it was two bus journeys from the Pentagon, whereas I only had to get to grips with one. Julia again:

The city is laid out quite sensibly in grid squares, but my feel for locality deserted me pro tem and I found it very confusing, not helped either by the fact that I had to change buses too on my way home. We would emerge from a rather chilly, air-conditioned Pentagon building to the underground bus station, where we were greeted by a blast of hot air and humidity, both at about ninety degrees, and generally a thunderstorm into the bargain. The first bus was owned by the state of Virginia and the passengers were segregated – white in front and Black people at the back – but I didn't really approve of this. The next, grander, bus was owned by the State of Washington DC and was much better, although I usually got carried miles past my stop and so saw a lot of Washington inadvertently. I eventually learnt my way around quite well.

The idea of learning my way around Washington by trial and error filled me with dread, especially as my duties sometimes involved being a Special Courier of secret papers from one department to another within Washington. I bought or was given a guidebook to Washington with a fold-out map and an essential 'Washington Street Arrangement' section, explaining the naming format of the street addresses. I was more confident about my delivery tasks once orientated with a basic understanding of the street structure, which was divided into four quarters. Each quarter was designated either northeast, northwest, southwest or southeast, and the streets running north and south were numbered (First, Second, etc.), while the east and west streets were designated with letters (F Street, G Street, etc.). Even with a better grasp of the geography of the city, I was always relieved to hand over the precious documents and there were still many times while out socially where I had no idea where I was or found myself at a location too far to walk home alone. Fortunately, there was always a friend or colleague happy to see me to the door of my hotel, which was listed in the guidebook as 'Cairo, 1615 Q St. N.W.'. I still have my guidebook and with the exception of the tattered front cover, it is in excellent condition, even the map.

CHAPTER 23

CITY LIFE

Writing a diary of my time in Washington was as prohibited as it was at Bletchley Park, but I reasoned a simple engagement diary would not break the rules if I kept the entries to a few words. The scribbles nestled between photographs the diary contained of the 'Masterpieces from the National Gallery of Art, Washington, DC' are so cryptic that all these years later it is hard to remember what they mean. Yet it is amazing that some prompts can lead to a flood of memories of long forgotten faces, places and experiences in my mind, while other entries remain obscured by the fog of time.

The engagement diary shows I embraced the social life in Washington almost immediately. There was so much to see and do with lots of new people to get to know. There were also some good old British traditions to follow, one of which was to sign the visitors' book at the Embassy. By way of acknowledgement, we all received visiting cards from His Majesty's Ambassador to Washington, at the time, Edward Wood, the first Earl of Halifax. I have kept mine along with other memorabilia, just to remind myself it happened.

I was delighted to bump into Miss de Freitas and her mother at the Cairo Hotel and also relieved to find out she made it to Washington no worse for a muddle of papers in London.

The many British personnel on duty in Washington integrated well with our American allies. I often took lunch with my American colleagues and we had the choice of where to eat as food was served in canteens as well as outside in the five-acre open-air area in the courtyard at the building's centre. This was the area where General Dwight Eisenhower drove round in a tank when he returned from Europe after the end of hostilities. Despite its size, the temperature of the central area took your breath away in contrast to the cool air-conditioned building, so I preferred to eat my lunch inside.

Of all the food I ate, I mostly remember the salads, which included watermelon. Although commonplace today, these salads were a complete luxury to me after all those years of rationing, which was minor in the US compared to the level I experienced at home. However, there was some rationing of meat, which was exchanged for small tokens. I wasn't the only one enjoying the food, Julia recalls putting on a stone in weight in the first few months from indulging in inch-thick fillet steaks, ice-cream and dining out.

There were no catering facilities at the Cairo Hotel, so all my meals were taken in cafés or restaurants. I paid forty-four dollars a month for my room and I was paid an extra five dollars a day for food, which was ample to cover my eating expenses. Food was not scarce; as soon as you sat down in the booth at a restaurant, a waitress would bring out a jug of water and a large lettuce leaf piled with cottage cheese to eat while you waited for the main course. I was also amused to discover that you could deposit a nickel in a slot and select a record to be played within the booth.

Off duty, I mostly mixed with British friends. We would eat out, go to cocktail parties at the flats of those fortunate to have them and attend concerts or the occasional ballet. I wore civilian clothes when off duty, which were cheap to buy, but did not seem to be made of the same quality as those I had at home. Not that I minded, as it was a pleasure to explore the department stores and browse among the wide selection of goods that were not available in the time of frugal rationing at home.

I got on well with my roommate Pip and we formed a strong bond over our cockroach annihilations. Pip had short dark hair and a pretty, friendly face, with a fun personality. We only met up in the evenings back at the hotel, as she did not work in the Pentagon. I know she was a Private in the ATS, but I did not know what she did in Washington.

I met up with Julia from time to time, and went to her billet for dinner and to listen to gramophone records then went to the drugstore for some ice-cream. In those days, we were advised not to go about unescorted in the evenings, so as the evening came to an end we went to 1733/9th Street and called on John Burrows. A thunderstorm cut short one evening, but John still escorted me to the Cairo Hotel. We were lucky with our men. Our chaps were very helpful in this and always made sure we were seen back to our billets. John, in particular, was very helpful, almost taking on the role of chaperone as well as being great company. There are multiple diary entries where I record lunch or some outing with John.

Julia didn't find her work too onerous and enjoyed Sunday as a day off every week, which she found odd after Bletchley's complicated rota system, where you could never guarantee that a day off would fall on a weekend. Her landlady, Elizabeth Jackson, took her tenants for Sunday drives around Maryland and Virginia in her ancient car.

In the autumn, I did manage to get away from the city for a weekend with my American friend (the one who checked my pass each morning at the office door). We travelled by train to her family home near Providence in Rhode Island. Again, the contrast with the train journeys I had taken in England was remarkable – there were no blackouts, no crowding or sleeping on the floor. We did have an uncomfortable situation with a drunken GI pestering us, but the train guard soon moved him so we were able to enjoy our journey in peace. I remember how beautiful the countryside looked in the rich autumn colours and the fields of ripening corn. We spent a fabulous weekend roasting marshmallows on the barbeque and taking a tour by car to explore a landscape untouched by war.

CHAPTER 24

LETTERS HOME

At the end of the war with Japan, I was working in a British Joint Services Mission office near the White House when I met Margaret Denniston, known as 'Y', who was the daughter of the former deputy head of the cypher school at BP, Commander Denniston. We became friends; the last time we met was in 2005, just before she died.

On the morning of 6 August 1945, the Americans dropped an atomic bomb on Hiroshima. The authorities had previously intercepted a message indicating that Japan would never surrender and the decision was then made to take this action, which finally turned the tide of war. On the 9 August 1945, a second bomb was dropped on Nagasaki. I will never forget hearing this news. Everyone in Washington (and no doubt the rest of the US) 'went crazy' – people blared their car horns continuously and tore around the city, shouting and waving. I joined a crowd thronging around the White House calling out, 'We want Harry' (Harry Truman, who was President of the US at the time). I didn't truly understand the impact the bomb would have on Japan, nor the lasting effects of radiation on future generations. At the end of a long war, all we understood was we were winning and on 14 August 1945 Japan finally surrendered. Only later did the horror of the devastation caused by the bombs sink in.

Steaks had been difficult to come by, but on the day the bombs were dropped, steaks appeared in the restaurants as if by magic. The celebrations went on all night; such excitement and the noise from hundreds of car horns drowning everything else.

My thoughts moved onto returning home and I was both excited and overwhelmed by all I had to do to get ready. I wrote home twice during this period and both letters bring back memories of excitement and anxiety.

August 22nd 1945
My darling Mummy,

Dorothea tells me you are still sane! That's good cos I'm beginning to wonder whether I still am ... There seems to be so much to do and so much to think about before coming home. I simply must see some more of the country and buy as much as possible. However, although everything seems on top of me at the moment, I don't suppose it will be so bad when it comes to the point.

I'm sending this over by a friend who is returning, so you should have it by the weekend. The weather is lovely now, still pretty hot but nothing like it was a month or so ago.

Aunt Lois hasn't answered yet but post is bad so no doubt I'll have to wait a bit.

On Monday (20th Aug) I sent off the parcel with a nightie and sundry oddments. I have no idea how long it is likely to take but do tell me when it arrives.

Things which were rationed and hard to get over here during the war are already coming back, so I hope in time to get fountain pens and all the other things we are in need of. It is really amazing – about 24 hours after the Japanese surrender, petrol could be bought ad lib. and most groceries off points. I shouldn't think there's much hope of seeing the end of rationing at home yet, is there?

Dorothea seems to have had a good holiday. Oh dear, I shall be so glad to get back Ma, there is so much indefinite news about demobbing that I don't feel very enthusiastic about work. Still I'm almost certain to be in England by Xmas if not demobbed. So I mustn't grumble. Actually I'm still enjoying myself and there's plenty of interest to do.

This notepaper is 'Office' and I don't suppose I should use it! So don't take any notice of the address at the top.

On reading this through I think it reflects my momentary bored and unsettled state. Sorry – hope the next one won't be so.

Much love to you all.
Your loving Betts

Monday 24 September 1945
My dearest Mummy,

Well, I'm really getting organised for my return – which, praise be, is now supposed to be October 5th (at least that's the sailing date). Please tell Daddy I have a watch for him – I'm mailing it! And I have a fountain pen, amongst other items for you.

Oh dear I'm in such an excited state. I feel quite incapable of writing a letter ...

Will send a cable from New York when I'm leaving.

Bye for now.
Your loving Charlotte

The heat and humidity of Washington made writing letters a challenging event and this letter did not fare well. The blue ink of the letter is smudged by droplets of sweat dripping from my hands as the fountain pen scratched across the page. I managed to keep my August letter free from water damage by tying a handkerchief around my wrist to catch any sweat trailing down my arm onto my hand, which is fortunate, because the thin, semi-transparent paper would likely have disintegrated with the wet.

While waiting for my movement order with instructions to return home, I continued working in the building near the White House to help out with general tidy-up duties. Security was still tight and if I went shopping at lunchtime I had to show the guards everything I had bought, which could be embarrassing if it involved personal items. It was also time to hand back the light Canadian uniform and return to my official ATS uniform in preparation for the return to England. I managed to hang onto the light stockings, which caused much envy when I finally returned home.

Those last days held opportunities to buy lots of clothes and gifts for my parents. I filled my two issue kit bags and also managed to obtain a further two kit bags, which seemed a good idea until I had to carry a bag under each arm and one in each hand upon arrival in New York.

CHAPTER 25

BACK TO BLETCHLEY

On the 4 October 1945, I finally received the movement order detailing our travel itinerary. As a Staff Sergeant, I was the most senior rank and was placed in charge of the other ATS women for the duration of the journey to England. They were Sergeants Auld (W/207714), Gillies (W/169125), Perkin (W/179286), Regan (W/46840) and Wheeler (W/35841); Corporals Lewis (W/61268) and Thompson (W/147702) and Lance Corporal Leith (W/265166). I am thankful that I had the foresight to keep my copy of the movement order typed on British Army Staff, Washington DC-headed paper and signed by the ATS Senior Commander at the BAS because it is a reminder of the details one so easily forgets after all these years.

1. *You will proceed to Union Station on Friday 5 October 45 to catch the 15.00 hrs train to New York.*
2. *On arrival in New York you will proceed to the Women's Military Services Club, 50th & Madison Avenue, where accommodation has been reserved for you.*
3. *You will report to B.A.S Movements Branch, 25 Broadway, New York, on Saturday 6 October 45, as per instructions given in embarkation orders held by you.*
4. *All luggage, with the exception of overnight bag, will be left at Penn Station on arrival in New York.*

On arrival in New York, we discovered the stevedores (porters) had gone on strike a week after a mass walkout of elevator operators, doormen, porters and others facilitating the movement up, down and around New York's high-rise commercial buildings. The strike over ongoing contract disputes was the start of many other worker strikes, including the stevedore strike, stranding us in New York. However, it gave us the opportunity to see something of New York, including a production of *The Importance of Being Earnest* put on by some local nuns who sounded more English than we did; it was hilarious. I also went to the ballet, *Ballet Russe Highlights*, choreographed by Léonide Massine. It was a collection of short ballet highlights, including a memorable one titled 'The Dentist'. The furious rain prevented me from really taking in the sights, but the unexpected stay in New York was very enjoyable and was made possible by an additional two-dollar allowance for the night of 5 October 1945 to supplement my usual five dollars North American Consolidated Allowance.

With no sign of a break in the strike, we made our way down to the Pier 90 North River on Sunday 7 October 1945 at 20.00 hours. The Embarkation Order reminded us that 'Conveyance of baggage to Pier is Officers' and Other Ranks' own responsibility, except those Other Ranks who are staged by No. 8 Battery, Maritime R.A.' Optimistically, it also states 'IMPORTANT On arrival at Pier, do not let your cabin baggage out of your sight, and retain your porter who will carry cabin baggage on board.'

With no porters to be retained, I lumbered to the ship with a case under each arm and one in each hand weighted down with my kit, gifts, clothes and essentials no longer available at home due to rationing. As we approached our ship, it was like we were the size of ants milling around an enormous shoe. The *Aquitania* was gigantic.

As I wobbled my way along the boarding gangway, I may have regretted my shopping expeditions, but these were forgotten as soon as I dropped the bags onto this once-luxurious Cunard Line transatlantic cruise ship with accommodation for 3,230 passengers. Once dubbed 'The Boat Beautiful', the *Aquitania* was now a scruffy requisitioned troop ship that had spent more of its thirty-six years of service requisitioned by the government than it had transporting leisure cruisers. Two years earlier, the *Aquitania* had delivered a contingent of the nineteen Americans of the 6813th Signal Security Detachment to serve Bletchley Park, one of whom was my friend Walter Sharp.

By the time I stepped on board, there was little sign of its former opulence, but it was taking me home and I spent most of the first two days sitting on deck enjoying the glorious weather. As there was still a risk of sailing through unexploded mines, however, it was impossible to relax completely, especially when the Atlantic turned nasty. For the remaining three days to Southampton, I was very sick and stayed below in very basic conditions. It was a great relief to disembark!

The police at Southampton kindly took me and the other ATS girls through a side door, thus avoiding Customs, and put us on a train for London, where I felt relieved to finally arrive at the holding unit at Radnor Place. In my excitement to be back, I thought of calling on my friend Angela Lenton. So I rushed into her office, only to find myself face to face with the former Prime Minister's daughter, Lady Mary Churchill, a Junior Commander in the ATS, who had been an administrative officer at the Radnor since September. She smiled sweetly as I backed out in embarrassment saying, 'Very sorry, Ma'am.'

From Radnor Place, I returned to Bletchley on 30 October 1945 to await a new posting, where I arrived as they were shredding paper and dismantling machinery.

I stayed at Shenley Road Military Camp at Bletchley for one or two nights, where I remember eating a meal. I was not required to help the few people left to pack up the site, so I felt a little lost and, it is sad to say, it was almost an anti-climax in comparison to the bustle and focus that had filled the place during the war years. I remember the atmosphere, which reminded me of the feeling one gets after everyone has gone home from a party or the sense of emptiness after packing up a house before a move. For me, the war was over, but at least I had one final stay at Bletchley Park.

Julia returned to England on the *Queen Elizabeth* and returned to Bletchley with the same feelings of anti-climax after the excitement of the US. I didn't see her; she would have been billeted in the locality. She remained working for Government Communications Headquarters checking through obsolete messages from French Indo-China until she married in early 1947.

CHAPTER 26

DEMOB

The act of being demobilised from the British army was not as simple as handing in my kit and waving goodbye. It was a lengthy process of waiting, letter writing, form filling, more waiting and, eventually, the discharge papers came through. I returned to England in October 1945, but was not demobbed until February the following year. No doubt the time it took to process the demobilisation of all those who enlisted before me was a key contributor to the length of my wait. After my final night at Bletchley Park, I was posted to No. 2 Eastern Command Holding Unit to wait for my discharge from the army. According to my service record I was back home within two weeks on the unemployed list for eight weeks on compassionate grounds due to Mother's health.

It gave me time to re-acclimatise to being back in England, after the noise and rush of Washington. I also had to adjust to rationing once again. Arriving in the US to see an abundance of food had been a joy after the rationing in England. Adjusting the other way round was less so.

While I was in Washington, the various teams at Bletchley Park received a word of thanks from their heads of section and it is a shame I didn't receive one for my section to retain as a keepsake. Copies of those written by other heads of sections survive in official records including one written on 10 July 1945, by John Herivel, who was then the head of the Newmanry at the Government Code and Cypher School, reminding his team of their duty to secrecy. He realised that our relief at the end of the war could make us less vigilant about the oath of secrecy we took on our first day in Bletchley Park, as we returned to our families and picked up the lives we had left behind in September 1939. He also had an eye on the future and a time when the secrecy was no longer needed:

Nothing left for me to say except Good Luck and Goodbye...
and this:

The Official Secrets Act will be rigidly enforced as long as there is any possibility of another war. But some of you, who live to be very old, may read one day, what the work in BP as a whole, of which yours was a vital part, really meant, not only to your own country, but to the world. And then you can be proud, and tell your grandchildren the story of the tapes that spun on silver wheels, and how the skill and determination of free men and women, guided by the light of reason freely used, helped to turn the evil tide of Fascist irrationalism and slavery in Europe.

J.W.J. Herivel

The newly named Government Communications Headquarters moved to its post-war home in Eastcote early in 1946. In August 1949 Nigel de Grey wrote an analysis of the success of the establishment during its war years and recommendations in the event of future conflicts in his *Memorandum by Mr de Grey*. It includes an assessment of the calibre of staff recruited from the Foreign Office and the three services during the war, dividing them into 'high-grade' codebreaking and technical staff who were educated to degree level (mostly men), and 'medium- and low-grade labour', describing everyone else.

By 'high grade', Mr de Grey was referring to those working on high-grade material such as Enigma and Lorenz. These were a 'team of young dons', all of them men as, he said, 'few women reached the highest levels'. As well as codebreakers, the team also comprised 'high-grade' intelligence officers (which he describes as partially created out of 'failed cryptanalysts'), linguists and traffic analysts, all of whom needed, 'some degree of puzzle mindedness'. The high-grade recruits posted in the Military Section were given army commissions, which enabled them to fit in to the military structure. He assesses the success of each of the channels of recruitment through universities/secondary schools, Foreign Office, Ministry of Labour, Civil Service Commission and the services. He wrote about recruitment through the services as:

There was never, except for the initial recruit mentioned in the first paragraph, any clear understanding about the staffing of the Service Sections or any uniformity of procedure between them. Everything tended to be done on a short-term solution of an immediate problem. Uniformed personnel worked under, over and with civilians in almost all sections. There was a great deal of give and take over this, rendered perhaps easier from the fact that there were very few regulars, almost all service personnel being war-entry. There were however occasional difficulties e.g. WAAF working under civilians in the T/P rooms. As time went on, so much of the educated classes was [sic] swept up by the Services that GC&CS had to press the

Services to comb out from Intelligence courses etc. suitable officers and linguists.

Occasionally, service feeling had to be pandered to, e.g. the Army and RAF were better content if the Advisers in Hut 3 were in appropriate uniform, even though their knowledge were [sic] no greater than civilians.

GC&CS policy veered between initially preferring civilians, lest the Services demand too great a say on the conduct of GC&CS, and later urging the Services to provide more people, it being understood as a sine qua non that they house and fed them, the former objection having been overcome. Otherwise by a gentleman's agreement each Service provided a large block of labour (1) the WRNS manned the Bombes (2) Army (ATS) provided the T/A (SIXTA), (3) RAF communications (WAAF).

Everyone else fell into Mr de Grey's medium- and low-grade labour category, of which he writes:

Initial mistake in this field was omission to look all along the production line and to provide as a result enough supporting staff to help the higher grades. With the larger numbers employed in GCHQ, the calculation in each branch of proportions between high, medium and low-grade required should present no problem ... An unusually high percentage of supporting staff were
(i) University trained
(ii) Higher School Certificate standard.

This in the Services applied to the WRNS and ATS in particular serving in sections where a high standard of mental agility was required. The teleprinter (WAAF) and cypher (civil) staff were the lowest form of life generally not up to school certificate standard. There was at this level also a lack of commercially trained leaders e.g. women who had run typing pools in banks and insurance companies, accustomed to organizing output up to a given rate per day or men who had been sub-managers with a team working under them. The bank clerks, while excellently methodical, did not entirely fill the bill. No emphasis was laid in recruiting upon obtaining this type. Time was wasted by 'talented amateurs'. Very many of the tasks were of a plain 'factory' type.

It was astonishing what young women could be trained to do, e.g. Fish and Bombe WRNS Typex operators, in an incredibly short time with wonderful accuracy, although quite untrained to use their hands or apply their minds to such work.

Once one gets over some of Mr de Grey's discourteous terms, it is interesting to read his assessment and see it from the viewpoint of the women in the services by those in charge. Once the war ended, we returned to our homes with instructions to forget what happened behind that perimeter fence in Bletchley, but for GCHQ as it became, it was necessary to take stock of the organisation's successes and failures with a view to learning from it as it stepped immediately into the Cold War.

His statement that, 'It is astonishing what young women could be trained to do' sums up the prevalent male view of the time; at least some women were able to exceed all expectations and were recognised for it. For most of the women at Bletchley Park, the compartmentalisation of work made it difficult for them to advance or move to a different section; transfers were more likely when removing a dud.

I feel very fortunate I was able to prove my worth and get the chance to do more meaty work. Right from the beginning, Major Tester gave me the opportunity to do more than register information on index cards, but my written German was not good enough. I can only assume he put in a good word for me when I was transferred into the Japanese Military Section because paraphrasing deciphered Japanese messages was completely different work and the officers in charge would have required reassurance I was up to the job. My selection to go to Washington was evidence to me I had done a good job, even though nobody tells one these things at the time. My attitude to get on with whatever is put in front of me without question and do it to the best of my ability stood me in good stead, as did the good fortune of working for some admirable men.

The only time I wavered in my resolve was crossing the stretch of sea in Poole to climb aboard the sailing boat whilst being violently ill from a mix of travel sickness and fear of my first flight and being confined in a small place with a group of men in civilian clothes. A uniform made me feel safe and it was frightening thinking I might give the game away.

On 23 January 1946 my temporary relegation to the unemployed list came to an end and I received an order to report to my commanding officer in six days' time at 4 pm, and a rail warrant from Ludlow to Lingfield in Surrey and a postal order for five shillings in advance of pay. I was required to apply to the local Employment Exchange for my unemployment insurance book to hand in at the time of rejoining and wait until demob at the end of February 1946.

CHAPTER 27

POST-WAR YEARS

Armed with a 'nest egg' of £52 and clothing coupons, I went back to the family smallholding, Ryecroft, to help out. The war years must have been a great strain on my parents, as they were for thousands of others of that age group. There was a collective air of sadness for the loss of loved ones, loneliness and uncertainty. Not to mention the daily struggle caused by food and fuel shortages.

My war years were relatively comfortable and interesting. Bletchley Park was for me the next best thing to attending university – exploring a new-found independence and living amongst a cross-section of interesting people. In my view, it was a unique establishment and a unique experience. I am sure such a gathering could never be repeated.

Life moved on and so did I. The government paid for my six-month secretarial course in London from late 1946 to Easter 1947. I secured digs with a Mr and Mrs Hancock in Croydon and became friends with their niece, Margaret Borthwick, and her husband, John.

According to an advertisement in the *Norwood News* on 15 January 1932, Grosvenor Secretarial College specialised in short diploma courses to prepare women for secretarial work. The curriculum covered shorthand, typing, a language of our choice (I took Spanish), how to write business letters and all the etiquette rules in connection with invitations and replies. We also received some guidance in stock market dealings (way over my head!) and I came away with my only qualification – a RSA 1st class in typing.

My cousin Rosemary Harris attended the same course and sailed through everything with top marks, as she always did, and with her degree in, I think, Latin and Greek, she soon had a job as personal assistant to the head of the National Institute of Research Dairying at Reading University, where she remained for forty-seven years, and was awarded an MBE for her work there.

It was a dreadful winter; everywhere was frozen up, and the food and fuel shortages remained in place until 1953. Some of my fellow students fainted from the cold. I dared to attend in a pair of army-issue trousers (dyed plum) and was sent for by the head. I was given a strict telling-off for appearing in such garb, which she described as 'quite unsuitable for young gentlewomen'. I pleaded with her, reminding her that travelling on an unheated train to and from Croydon each day warranted some protection. I got away with it, on the understanding that the minute the weather improved, a skirt would be worn.

The head of the secretarial course was not the only person to comment on my wardrobe choices. My father was incredulous at my decision to wear high heels, calling them ridiculous when I tottered behind him along the ice-covered lane to the bus stop. I was determined to wear them after a wartime of beetle-crushing army shoes and struggled on regardless.

Adjusting to the post-war years was difficult. It had been a relief to go home because it was the end of the war, but there is no denying that life felt flat after all the demands of work, the distractions of the social scene, and the noise and novelty of Washington. Many people picked up where they left off with work, training or education, while others had to find a way to readjust.

I returned home to Ryecroft at the end of my secretarial course and slipped back into my old life. I began to wonder if the time away had been little more than a dream. I helped Mother out with the garden and the animals and I did not mind; it was a relief to ease her burden. I also helped in one most unexpected way – Mother loved my ATS knickers. She wore them while feeding the animals and claimed they were very comfortable and useful. She was welcome to them!

For the next three years, I helped on the smallholding, sat with my parents in our seat in the church and cycled round the village on a bicycle, much in the same way I had as a teenager. It wasn't the bicycle with the wooden seat, and my Bletchley bicycle had been stolen during the war, so I must have acquired it locally upon my return.

My sister Margaret and I became part of the 'Little Orchestra' in Ludlow, conducted by Ludwig Otto Gerhard Haase, known as Gerhard. He had been Luftwaffe ground crew, but was captured in Holland in 1944 and transferred to Camp 84, a prisoner-of-war work camp at Sheet Farm in Ludlow. He and the other German prisoners were all artists of one sort or another and had no interest in being in the German army. One of the prisoners gave us some of his paintings of the local area, one of which hung on my dining room wall for many years before I donated it to a local museum. Gerhard remained in Ludlow to marry one of the orchestra members, Nan Chesters, in 1952 and trained as an accountant.

For me, those initial post-war years held another obstacle. Due to my obligations under the Official Secrets Act, I was not allowed to tell any prospective employer what I had been doing during the war years, beyond saying I was a clerk in the ATS. I did have a written testimonial entered on Part II of a 'Notification of Impending Release' form submitted to the officer in charge of the record office. The ATS, then WRAC, must have used the wording on this statement in letters of reference to potential employers:

Military Conduct: Exemplary.

Testimonial: Has held a position of trust & responsibility. Cheerful & willing & most reliable. Works well with her contemporaries.

Armed with a service trade of Clark, Special Intelligence Division, Class I and a typing qualification, I knew I had to get a job. I had no plans for a career in a particular field, just the knowledge that I had to work and earn a wage.

In April 1950, I finally found employment as Assistant Matron at St Monica's Training College, Cheltenham, which I think was for trainee nursery nurses. It was a live-in post and I was responsible for ordering food supplies, arranging meals and ensuring all the domestic arrangements had been carried out by the cleaning staff. It was horrid, I disliked the work enormously and left in December of the same year to return home to Richard's Castle. I managed to put my secretarial training to good use in my next post at Ludlow Grammar School. Luckily, the then head of the school had been posted to Bletchley Park during the war and understood immediately that

I could not divulge details. It was a case of 'who you know' as distinct from 'what you know' on that occasion and I had no difficulty in getting the temporary post on the office staff.

Years later, my American friend from Bletchley, Walter Sharp, wrote that he too experienced difficulty finding his first job after the war. He applied for a post teaching maths at an engineering school, but could not disclose what he did in the war, although he did eventually admit the work he had done was 'technical'. After a year, he went to work at the National Security Agency (NSA) where his interviewer would have been more aware of the need for discretion.

My post at Ludlow Grammar School came to an end after a few months, when the permanent secretary returned from illness. I enjoyed the work and would have stayed if I could, but at least I now had a job reference I could include on an application form and talk about during an interview.

Then, by chance, I stumbled on a job with Messrs Williams & Williams, a metal window manufacturers in Chester, where John Borthwick was managing director. I began there in August 1952 as part of a team of five secretaries, where I mainly dealt with staff pensions. I moved into an upstairs flat at 12 Glan Aber Park, Chester, a semi-detached house on a leafy suburban road located south of the river. The rest of the house was occupied by a delightful family. I don't remember their names; only that the man worked as a grocer in Chester.

You never knew when you were going to bump into someone who worked at Bletchley Park and Chester was no different. I met and became friends with June Rosina Solloway (nee Collins) who worked in Hut 5 at

Bletchley Park. Encouraged by June's husband, who was a member of the 4th Battalion, the Cheshire Regiment of the Territorial Army (TA), I joined the 321 (Cheshire Battalion) WRAC (TA) in January 1955 and became a commissioned officer after three months. I had to set aside one evening a week for my duties within the TA and two weeks for the annual camp.

My employer was in favour of the TA, so was happy to give me time off with pay to attend the annual TA camps. We shared the drill hall in Volunteer Street, Chester, with the Cheshire Regiment and were welcomed in their Officers' Mess. They were a jolly crowd of men, mostly local solicitors, land agents and other professions, so the social life was good – lots of cocktail parties and dances, and the great occasion when Her Majesty Queen Elizabeth presented new colours to the 4th and 7th Battalions on the Chester racecourse in 1957. She seemed so small surrounded by a crowd of tall men and it was the first of several occasions when I didn't quite meet the Queen. A splendid evening ball followed the ceremony, which went on till 4 am.

My main hobby at that time was badminton and I enjoyed arranging the matches. I also played some tennis, and music was still a big part of my life. I wasn't playing an instrument at this time, but joined the Deeside Orpheus Music Society instead. I have a black and white photograph of our production in October 1954 of *The Desert Song* in October 1954, which was a musical play by Sigmund Romberg popular with drama groups at that time. It was the first time our group had put on a full musical production with costumes and scenery as they usually opted for concert versions of musical plays. Like many of the performers, it was my first time on stage in front of an audience and I wore a beautiful patterned dress with collar, short sleeves and a full swing skirt, which was the fashion at the time. The music critic of the *Chester Chronicle* reported the five set changes were well managed and the scenery 'ingeniously devised', especially in light of the limited space backstage at the Assembly Rooms on Newgate Street. He praised the performance, our enthusiasm and the hard work of the entire crew. It was great fun.

In autumn 1958, I became a Permanent Staff Officer (PSO) in my battalion with the rank of Captain, Adjutant to the Commanding Officer Major Margaret Southern, and stayed there until the re-organisation of the TA in 1960. My position was to be discontinued on re-organisation so I was invited to apply for a short service commission. The Assistant Director of the WRAC gave me a reference on 30 November 1960.

Captain Vine-Stevens has been the full time adjutant of the WRAC (TA) battalion in Chester since November 1958. I therefore know her fairly well. She is energetic, loyal and hardworking, and is sound and well balanced. She has a fairly wide selection of outside interests. In tackling the job of adjutant, with no previous experience of full time commissioned rank, she has showed herself willing and capable of learning quickly by her mistakes, and she has steadily gained in knowledge and stature. She has considered carefully the very definite disadvantages of being commissioned in the rank of 2/Lt at the age of nearly 38, after holding the rank of Captain in the TA for two and a half years, and I think she has sufficient flexibility of mind and character to cope. She is young in outlook for her age.

What a hoot to think an age of thirty-seven was viewed as a potential detriment to the posting. People used to comment that I looked young for my age, to which I replied, well how should I look? I think the Assistant Director was correct – it is all about having a young outlook.

The 319, 320 and 321 Battalions amalgamated in 1961 with its headquarters in Southport. It was all very sad and I hated Southport.

Mother was very ill by this time but came to visit me in Southport and must have had an idea that her time was short to take the trouble to travel so far to see me. Perhaps she thought it was a final farewell. A few weeks later I was in Scotland at Camp near Gleneagles when I received a message to get home immediately. I raced off to the train and arrived at Hereford General Hospital with just enough time to see her before she died. I later discovered that the man who had taken the message had not passed it on with the urgency in which it had been sent. I doubt if she knew I was there and Daddy and Margaret had been with her, but I do not think I could have coped had I not been there for her final moments.

We were all shattered by Mummy's death – I had no idea how to come to terms with life without her. My grief was not helped by the new Commanding Officer's unsympathetic response to my tears, '*I didn't cry when my mother died*' she said. I wasn't sure how to respond to that. Dad's distraught state convinced me to request a posting to Bristol, which made it easier to get to my father's home, Monkerton House near Leominster, to give him moral support when I had time off. He was totally 'lost' without Mummy, but insisted I should carry on with my life in the army. Life does have to go on; we have no choice.

During my years as a full-time TA officer, I met people from all walks of life from the very humblest to the very highest in society. I was apprehensive when faced with meeting the 10th Duke and Duchess of Beaufort in the sixties. They were both very active in the Bristol area and the Duchess became our Honorary Colonel (71 Bristol Coy WRAC (TA)). In this role, she visited our premises and the Mess, and hosted the company at Badminton House in Gloucestershire for a training weekend. I slept in a brass bedstead with a red silk bedspread and woke up to walls adorned with photos of the Duke in his Eton days.

I was intimidated at first, but need not have been worried. The Duke and Duchess were very easy to talk to and kind hosts. I will never forget the Duchess reminding me that the collective noun for goldfinches was a 'charm of goldfinches'. On another occasion, she joined us at TA camp in Folkestone and I asked her if she would like breakfast in bed, to which she replied, 'Oh no, Betty. Thank you. I hate crumbs in bed!' The Duchess presented all the officers with a shield when the company was disbanded in 1966. My shield is in my hall display of memories and mounted above my 'Bletchley – Freedom of the Park' parchment.

At the other end of the scale were some of the people I enlisted into the Regular WRAC and Queen Alexandra's Royal Army Nursing Corps whilst working as a recruiting officer for the West Midlands between 1966 and 1969. I interviewed the applicants in Birmingham, Stoke-on-Trent (Hanley), Shrewsbury, Worcester, Hereford, Wolverhampton and Coventry – a very mixed bag of accents and attitudes, rich and poor, educated and not so. The skills I developed during my time at Bletchley,

Washington and in the army enabled me to communicate and engage with these recruits with respect and compassion. I may not remember all their names like I remember the Duke and Duchess, but my time helping them decide on their futures was more rewarding. Not bad for someone who stood in shock at an ATS training camp that autumn day in 1941 taking in the heady mix of women from differing backgrounds. It is all those experiences that made me good at my job and I never forgot the value of discretion.

I drove from Birmingham to all the towns in my recruiting area on a weekly basis. I enjoyed driving when I was in the army and never minded travelling long distances, but I still enjoyed the times when the army allocated a driver to chauffeur me between recruitment centres. It amuses me now to think that my application to join the ATS as a driver was turned down during the war on the basis that I didn't have a licence, when my second career in the army involved so much driving.

From the 1940s to the present day, I have watched the growth of some of our major road developments from behind the wheel of a variety of vehicles, particularly the ring roads in Birmingham and the M6, M5 and M42 motorways. I often joke that I know every pothole between home and Bletchley Park. I find the road very hazardous these days, with the volume of traffic and some drivers' lack of consideration and sense of danger. I have to rely on friends and family to drive me long distances, but I still navigate the roads around my village from behind the wheel most days.

CHAPTER 28

A WALK DOWN THE AISLE

One day in 1968, I drove to Shirley in the borough of Solihull in the West Midlands, determined to find a garage to park my car at night. I found a block of garages for rent and knocked on the door to enquire about terms. A young man opened the door and introduced himself as Colin Webb. Suddenly his father appeared and announced he would handle it and that was how I met my husband, Alfred Webb. I was in uniform, which drew his attention and we began to share stories of our time in the war. Needless to say, I was still bound by my oath of silence about the work, so gave the usual vague response about clerical work. He had served in the Guards Armoured Division, which was formed in 1941 to provide a much-needed defensive force on home soil. I am not sure what he was doing before this, except that he was one of those dealing with the aftermath of the Coventry bombing in November 1940. He did not share the details, other than to say the devastation was distressing to witness. The Guards Armoured Division served in Europe from June 1944 as part of the troops sent into France after the first wave of D-Day troops landed in Normandy.

We hit it off straight away and romance soon blossomed. We went out shooting with his springer spaniel, Prince, who was trained to the gun, and he was a keen cricketer and a member of Blossomfield Cricket Club in Solihull, where we socialised with friends.

One evening, we stopped at a pub for a drink. My usual tipple of choice was a gin and tonic and Alfred enjoyed a pint of beer. All of a sudden, he proposed. Alfred was not a man for public displays of affection, so there would not have been any hand-holding and certainly nothing as excessive as getting down on one knee to ask for my hand in marriage. Needless to say, I was taken aback for a moment, but I had no hesitation in saying yes.

The engagement ring came later from Alfred's jeweller friend, who could get a good discount. It is a beautiful sapphire ring that has stood the test of time and I wear it every day.

Although we were nearing fifty, Alfred was a man of tradition and asked my father to give his permission for us to marry. I had nothing to worry about; they had previously bonded over a mutual love of cricket and my father gave his blessing.

Alfred knew how unhappy I was in my current job. I had resigned from the army in September 1969 for a post as Area Secretary to the Young Women's Christian Association (YWCA). The army did not contribute to pensions of Territorial commissions at that time, only to those in the regular army, and I was starting to think ahead to how I would manage in retirement. The move turned out to be a disaster and I gave it up on marriage.

Alfred and I married on 18 July 1970 in Leominster on a lovely sunny day, with a small party of family and friends in the garden of my father's home nearby.

Alfred wore a dark suit with grey tie and white carnation in his buttonhole. I have always loved wearing colourful clothes so chose a jacquard pink dress with scalloped collar, wide-brimmed hat and three tiers of pearls Alfred gave to me as a wedding gift. The dress still hangs in my wardrobe and the pink is as vibrant as the day of the wedding.

For our honeymoon, Alfred, Prince and I motored to Yorkshire for a week of walking and sightseeing. On our return we turned our attention to a new home and bought a large but rather neglected house in Redditch, Worcestershire for approximately £25,000. We named it 'Redwing' after seeing a redwing bird land in the garden at Dad's house just at the time we were trying to think of a name. The house has retained the name to this day.

Alfred restored our house into a comfortable home during a time when Redditch was undergoing vast development to ease the population overflow of Birmingham. It is a shame the development didn't extend to our kitchen, which was tiny for the size of the house. With that exception, I was happy with the house and its position along an old road on the northeastern edge of the town centre where the Victorian terraced houses ended and a comprehensive school and larger interwar houses lined the road. Our house backed onto open fields with views out towards Birmingham so it did not feel too built up until groundwork for a new dual carriageway sliced across the landscape near to the house.

They were good years for me, but very different from all the varied experiences of my previous life. I found being a housewife isolating. Cleaning, shopping, washing, cooking – all vital chores but such a bore when they are the most consuming part of the day. I had been in work since 1941 and my jobs were all about people and travelling to meet people.

One day I discovered I wasn't the only one keeping a secret. I came home from Birmingham and, waiting to catch the bus home, I saw Alfred across the street leaving the doctor's surgery. I went over and blurted out, 'What are you doing here?' Then he told me: he had advanced hardening of the arteries. He had been unwell for some time, but did not want me to worry. It was 1976 and Alfred was only fifty-seven.

Nonetheless, he continued to work full time as a manager at Weaver Brothers, a construction company in the neighbouring town of Bromsgrove. William Weaver started the company in 1865 and it remained a family-run firm until William's three great-grandsons retired in 2001. During the war, the company won a contract to build War Department wireless transmitting stations and I imagine this sort of work appealed to Alfred when he joined the firm. As his condition worsened, he spent more time at home, so I had to look for work. By good fortune, I opened one of the Birmingham newspapers and saw a vacancy with Birmingham Law Society, a large regional society representing those working in the legal profession in Birmingham and the Midlands. I went for the interview in an office in an old building covering four floors in Temple Street and started soon after in a short-term post helping the social secretary put together a social event. It transpired that there was vacancy for a new administrative secretary, so I put in for the job and was successful.

It was a challenge to work full time again and manage the household, but I didn't mind the hectic dash to fit everything into the day. I wish the circumstances of my return to work had been different, but I was delighted, nonetheless, to be back in the bustle of a busy office and the distraction helped me manage my worry about Alfred.

He began to work fewer hours, but was a proud and independent man who did not like to be idle. He remained part of the Blossomfield Cricket Club in Solihull, and he helped out where he could at home with the domestic chores and cooking. He was adamant I was unable to choose a good cut of meat, so I let him sort it out.

All too soon the doctors told Alfred the only chance to prolong his life was to undergo an operation to remove both legs. Stubborn and determined, he struggled on until he had to accept the inevitable. He even went to work on the morning before he was admitted to the Queen Elizabeth Hospital in Birmingham. The medics did all they could to keep him alive, but it was not to be. With hindsight, I think Alfred would have struggled to adapt to life as an amputee, but at that time I believed we would find a way to cope. When Alfred passed away on 2 March 1978, I was devastated. We had only nine and a half years together.

CHAPTER 29

RENEWED INDEPENDENCE

I took a month off work after Alfred's death, but it took me a long time to come to terms with life without him. Colin, Alfred's son from a previous marriage, and his family lived nearby and were a great comfort, as were his other sons Ian, Pete and their families. I am very lucky to have shared happier times since then with my extended family, which has extended into several new generations.

Fortunately, Birmingham Law Society kept my job open for me and I stayed happily employed with them for sixteen years as administrative secretary with a staff of twelve and a responsibility to the council. I also found new hobbies, including weekly Norwegian lessons given by a Mrs Veslemoy Lunt, whose husband Canon Ronald Lunt was head of King Edward's School in Birmingham.

The Norwegian lessons introduced me into another interesting mix of people – some with direct Norwegian connections, others, like me, just learning Norwegian and Norwegian culture simply because we were interested. I learnt that the Lunts first met in Norway in the early days of the war when the Canon was parachuted in with our forces. I also met ex-Bletchley Wren Joan Martin during the class. Her son and his Norwegian wife were members of a choir in their hometown of Straume, near Bergen. We entertained them when their choir visited Birmingham and I made more friends. One of the families hosted me in Norway in 1992 and I still write to them at Christmas time.

Norway is beautiful and I'm glad I was able to speak a little Norwegian, as I felt those we came in contact with were pleased to hear some of the English making an effort! In my view, to say English is spoken everywhere you go is neither true nor the right attitude. We are lazy about learning other languages. It is a pity because this attitude means we miss out on so much. When people ask me, 'Why Norwegian?' my reply is usually 'Why not?' I find it fascinating, although its similarity to German sometimes gets me into trouble with Norwegians, who understandably prefer not to be associated with their one-time invaders.

All through my working life since joining the ATS in August 1941, I have wondered how I would be 'rated' by others for not having had conventional schooling. 'PNEU home-school' doesn't always mean anything to most people unless fully explained. However, I believe there are a small minority of people who were educated thus and, like me, have managed to cope. Despite my worries and something of an inferiority complex, I succeeded in staying with various employments and generally 'holding my own' socially. To this day, my heart always sinks when someone says 'Do you remember how it was at school?' But now I have plucked up courage to say 'No, I do not, because…'

After the war, John Burrows became a school inspector in Norwich, Darlington and London. He was appointed Chief Inspector of Schools for the Department of Education and Science in the 1960s and was awarded a CBE in the year he retired, 1973. He had become a lay

Methodist preacher after the war and taught poetry and history to adult learners after retiring. After his wife, Enid, died in 1986, I motored up to his home in Ratby in Leicester to see him. We met up a few times after that and he came to Worcestershire in September 1995. I showed him my village, Wythall, including a jolly tour of the local transport museum. He wrote a touching thank-you letter when he arrived home that evening to say our reminiscing had stirred up some vivid memories of the people we worked with in Washington while other memories were lost in the mists of time. I could tell him now those mists become denser with every year.

John died peacefully at home in Ratby on 28 August 2008 at the age of 96. I went to his funeral at the Ratby Methodist Church on 4 September of that year. I have kept the order of service with its striking photograph of John sitting at his desk surrounded by papers, with a pen between his fingers. He could well be marking someone's schoolwork. The photographer has caught him in laughter and it is a fitting way to remember him.

My Spanish has been quite useful, reading the Spanish edition of the Organisation of American States magazine, shopping in Spain and Tenerife and trying to understand my Chilean hairdresser I used while there. I must say that was the most difficult! To me, the Chilean Spanish has quite a dialect, so I welcomed the opportunity to have another chance at improving my language skills later during a month's stay in Chile with relatives. In 1999, I travelled from Heathrow to Santiago, Chile, which took twenty-two hours. Admittedly there was a two-hour wait in Madrid, but even so, it was a very long journey. I spent a month in Chile with my cousin Josie and her husband, Marco Garido, in their beautiful home in Linderos, not far from Santiago. It was heaven. Beautiful trees and shrubs surrounded their bungalow, and they grew every fruit and vegetable you can imagine. They also had two dogs (Daisy and Tyson), a horse, chickens and several acres of arable land. There was no street lighting, so the night sky was perfect.

I felt a small earthquake one night, but there was no damage. We enjoyed walking in the foothills of the Andes with a crowd of local botanists, although Josie and I became separated from the main party and almost lost our way and had visions of spending the night surviving on the water in the little stream nearby. Luckily, we did find our way back safe and sound.

I gained enormous confidence during 2005 and 2006, being thrown in at the deep end as 'consort' to my friend Jill Dyer, who was chairman of our district council and, therefore, I accompanied her to a great number and variety of civil, social and business functions – about 150 in all. This was a most interesting and rewarding experience, and a great privilege and honour. The highlight of the year was attending a garden party at Buckingham Palace on 19 July 2005. We were chauffeur-driven to London in a luxurious official car and after a delicious lunch at the Goring Hotel in Beeston Place, we joined the crowd of nine and a half thousand people in the gardens at the rear of the palace. Entrance is through the palace, passing through the ballroom. Everyone was obliged to verify their identity to the guards by showing their passports, driving licences and a recent bill that included their full name and address. Afternoon tea consisted of beautifully presented sandwiches, cakes, ice-cream and iced coffee or other non-alcoholic beverages served by faultless young men and women in immaculate dress.

The guests were also very formally dressed – the ladies in fabulous colours and, of course, hats, the men in either military uniforms or morning dress, with chains of office where appropriate. All added to the spectacle. Her Majesty Queen Elizabeth, Prince Philip, the Duke of Kent, His Majesty King Charles and the Queen Consort in their roles as Prince Charles and the Duchess of Cornwall, and the Duke of York mingled with the guests. Sadly, because of the numbers, we did not see Her Majesty at close quarters.

Jill encouraged me to run for office on the parish council and I served Wythall Parish Council for thirty-two years. I enjoyed it for a long time, and it kept me occupied. I particularly enjoyed the period I was mostly concerned with the local footpaths and bridleways. I worked with volunteers to clear the routes and found it rewarding. I volunteered for a long period to do Meals on Wheels and Books on Wheels to support those in need within the community. Even now, I take part in community activities including a dementia café at the village hall.

I have been surprised and delighted that so many local groups of one sort and another have invited me to speak to them about my time at Bletchley Park and its war-time function. Giving these talks is most enjoyable for me and I am impressed by the amount of genuine interest in the subject.

It was not easy to talk about Bletchley Park at first, even after the veil of secrecy was lifted in July 1975. But I am grateful for the encouragement of a friend, in about 1994, to give talks about my war experiences and I gradually started to open up. My first talk to the Probus Club, to which my friend was affiliated was a hit. Since then I have talked to many groups, usually of about thirty to forty people, but sometimes to more than a hundred people at a time. From retired people to school children, it seems Bletchley Park has captured the imagination of the nation. I not only talk about Bletchley's past, but its evolving future as a museum that is open to the public. New information regularly comes to light from veterans and documents released into the National Archives, further enriching Bletchley's story.

CHAPTER 30

ONE THING LEADS TO ANOTHER

On 9 October 2009, a little over sixty years since my October return to England from Washington, I was honoured to attend Bletchley Park as one of the thirty-five veterans invited to attend the ceremony to celebrate the new commemorative badge awarded to all the surviving Bletchley Park veterans. Presented by the then Foreign Secretary, David Miliband, it was truly a day to remember. It filled me with pride to know that I had served my country in a way that is honoured and remembered today and will continue to inspire future generations.

It was the start of a new life for me. When I was preparing to settle down to the slow decline of inactivity of life in my mid-eighties, the story surrounding Bletchley Park captured the public's imagination and I became busier than ever in my effort to promote the story of Bletchley Park during the Second World War and highlight the hard work of the people who have helped it become a world-class museum and archive.

To date, I have given some two hundred talks about my time at BP to various groups, clubs and schools, which I find very rewarding. Most of the talks have been in the West Midlands, but I have been chauffeured to many places throughout the country to all sorts of events as speaker or as a guest of honour. I think the years I spent talking to potential army recruits has been good training for these events and I have never lost my enjoyment of speaking with people from all walks of life.

The audiences want to know about the purpose of the Government Code and Cypher School and are particularly fascinated by how its employees lived during the wartime conditions, asking questions about our duties, what we did for recreation, our living arrangements, friendships, marriages, etc. I think of every person in the audience as a future visitor at Bletchley Park and welcome any opportunity to spark the interest of someone new. It may seem self-indulgent to share some of the extraordinary events I have had the honour of attending, but I see it as a tribute to the organisations that arrange these events and the people who attend them. Every time a programme is repeated on television or someone remembers an event they attended and tells others, this could lead to more people visiting BP.

In March 2012, I was one of six veterans chosen to attend a dinner prepared by the *MasterChef* team. The event was recorded in March and those who took part were asked to keep it a 'secret' until it was shown on television in September that year. Our discipline in keeping secrets came in handy once again. A taxi served as our transport and, after a champagne reception, we moved into the library when the dinner was served by the three *MasterChef* finalists.

In addition to showing the chefs at work, the television programme gave a short history of each veteran's wartime role at Bletchley Park, with photographs taken at the time. Mine omitted Major Tester's name, which I am sad about, as he was one of the important figures at the time. It was a memorable occasion, with good food and much hilarity amongst the guests. They always enjoy hearing about the ATS khaki knickers!

The then Foreign Secretary William Hague's visit to Bletchley Park in 2012, when he announced government funding for the renovation of the huts, was another occasion to which I was invited with six other veterans. Lord Asa Briggs, Baroness Jean Trumpington, Captain Jerry Roberts, Gwendoline Page, Jean Valentine and I were presented to Mr Hague, who subsequently sent me a copy of his speech with a personal handwritten covering letter. How proud am I?

The audience also included Sir Iain Lobban, the then Head of GCHQ; Gordon Corera, the BBC's defence correspondent, and the Bletchley Park trustees. Lord Hague was presented with a refurbished Enigma machine, which went on display in the Foreign Office.

During the refreshment breaks we veterans had a jolly time reminiscing. Even though we didn't know each other during the war, we still had much in common and there is a wonderful bond between us.

The Bletchley Park Trust team headed by CEO Iain Standen are always so welcoming and interested in our wartime work there. I am sure that their hard work and genuine interest is just what is needed to keep Bletchley Park as a world-class heritage attraction.

Then came another totally unexpected invitation to tell my story to the people from Bremont, who made a limited edition watch called Codebreaker that has within it tiny pieces of wood from Hut 6. The exciting aspect of this is that Bremont donated part of the proceeds from the sale of the watches to Bletchley Park. I was honoured to be invited to the launch of the watch, hosted by Nick and Giles English, the co-founders of Bremont. I, along with other veterans Captain Jerry Roberts, Ruth Bourne and Jean Valentine, was warmly welcomed and had a super time.

The guests showed much interest in our wartime work, men and women two or three generations younger than I am and who had only heard about the Second World War from their parents and grandparents. I was pleased to realise the respect with which they held us. I often wonder how anyone born after 1945 envisages how we lived through the war years and how those times influenced our way of life thereafter.

And there is more! An invitation came from Bletchley Park to take part in the *Great British Railway Journeys* to be shown on television in early 2014. I drove down to Bletchley on a bitterly cold day and met with the producer, Tom Richardson. Perhaps this preliminary session was to decide whether I would be suitable to be filmed with Michael Portillo? To my delight, I was. So another trip to Bletchley Park and we gathered in the ballroom, where the stage was set for afternoon tea with Michael Portillo. We drank endless cups of tea as Michael questioned me about my service during the war. I only wish he hadn't topped mine with so much milk, as it was rather cool by the time I stopped talking long enough to drink it.

That year was busy as I was a guest of author Tessa Dunlop during the promotion of her book The Bletchley Girls. Tessa interviewed me and Doris Moss, who escaped Belgium with her sister and came to work at Bletchley Park, at BBC Salford. I was amused at the start of a telephone interview Tessa and I did with a radio programme, when Tessa announced 'Hello, I'm in bed.' Pat and Jean Owtram, who intercepted the German messages during the war, and I accompanied Tessa on a whirlwind visit to the Edinburgh Fringe Festival for another question and answer session. It was a shame there was no time to take in the rest of the festival.

There have been some unusual events during the last few years, including an interview by a robot from the Netherlands, which would use artificial intelligence to determine the next question based on my answer to its first one. Unfortunately, it did not go to plan, but it was interesting to watch modern technology take on the electro-mechanical Bombe machine, designed by Alan Turing and Gordon Welchman to reduce the time it took to find the settings of the Enigma machine during the war.

In 2017 a trip to Bletchley Park was a rollercoaster event when the wheelchair I was using in the lead-up to a hip operation and I were hoisted as one onto the lawn in front of the Mansion for an interview with Paul Martin for BBC's *Flog It!*. Then in 2019, I was one of five veterans taking part in live painting events at the National Army Museum for the 'Rise of the Lionesses' exhibition. It was a strange experience to be interviewed on stage while artist Ann Witheridge painted my portrait.

Not all memorable events were planned. In 2017, I was enjoying a day out at Bletchley Park to see some of the new exhibitions I rarely get time to see when I am there for a specific event. The trip coincided with a VIP visit by the Director of the National Intelligence Centre of Spain, General Félix Sanz Roldán. Surrounded by officials from MI5, MI6 and GCHQ, I greeted him in Spanish to his delight and we had a pleasant chat about my time at Bletchley Park. The annual Bletchley Park veterans' reunions have been a wonderful opportunity to meet others who worked at Bletchley Park and its outstations during the war. I have made some good friends at these events. We may only have met in our eighties and nineties, but our bond through Bletchley Park transcends the time in between. It is always enlightening to hear how the war changed people's lives and their outlooks.

During the 2011 reunion, my book *Secret Postings* was launched in a marquee in the Bletchley Park grounds. Ann and George Keller from the US bought a copy and came over again in 2012 to buy another. George is a US Navy veteran and he invited me to submit my wartime story in *Cryptolog*, the US Naval Cryptologic Veterans Association's magazine. This I did and, to my amazement, it appears in the Summer 2013 edition. They then went on to publish other articles of mine and a review of my book in subsequent editions.

CHAPTER 31

PANDEMIC

I have lived alone since Alfred died in 1978 yet I have never been lonely because I have always followed my mother's footsteps by keeping busy and finding interests to pursue. Email and video calls keep me connected to the wider world from my living room and there are family lunches, visitors for tea, a Saturday morning ladies' group and monthly WRAC meeting I attend. My work as a parish councillor that I did into my early nineties also took up a lot of time.

It has always suited me to keep my independence and even now at ninety-nine as I write this book, I still clean my bungalow. There are many challenges, for example it is hard to reach all the cobwebs, but I have come to an agreement with my spidery house guests. Changing the cover on the duvet requires endurance and some tasks must be carried out in stages. It helps that I try not to drop too many crumbs. Manufacturers don't have the elderly in mind when they make products, so even a small box of washing powder is heavy to lift and a screw-top lid is impossible. I am afraid I am beginning to lose the battle with the weight of a boiled kettle. I tackle these challenges with determination, but it is with great regret that I can no longer tend my garden and now employ a gardener. I am thankful to be physically able to care for myself with a little help from friends and family. With the exception of remembering names, my memory is not too bad either.

With things becoming more challenging at home, I viewed the news of the coronavirus with worry. How would I cope being confined to barracks? My neighbours dropped off food items at the front door and I added things I needed to a friend's online supermarket order, but for most food items, I telephoned an order through to the local butcher and they delivered it to the door. This reminded me of Messrs Stephens, the grocer in Ludlow from my childhood and the orders he took one week and delivered the next. So the domestic arrangements settled into an orderly routine reasonably well. My neighbours and I also started to sit on our adjoining garden walls for short spells and call across the shrubbery to one another in a loud, socially distanced and very communal conversation. We had a common enemy and it brought us together among the horror and the grief of those early days of the virus.

Then something quite extraordinary happened. The telephone rang and it was a journalist wishing to ask me questions about my time at Bletchley Park for an article to be published on or around the 75th anniversary of the end of the Second World War. No sooner had I arranged one interview and the telephone would ring with another request, then another. There were requests for the anniversary of VE Day, another for Victory over Japan (VJ) Day. Each request led to a series of further calls to set up the interviews and run tests for virtual interviews recorded over the internet. I was already familiar with one well-known video calling service, but I had to learn another. Then there was the time to prepare and then the time for the interviews and, I can honestly say, I have never been busier than in the first few months of the pandemic. The interview most people mention is the one in the *National Geographic* magazine because I am on the front cover wearing a red suit with my handbag on my lap. I can't quite believe it.

I feel fortunate that I had such a wonderful community on my doorstep and an enjoyable distraction to get me through the first lockdown. It seems that the public appetite for wartime stories about Bletchley Park continues to increase and there is always a telephone or video call to take, a talk to deliver or an event to attend. I will continue for as long as I can.

The most extraordinary event of the pandemic was the surprise arrival of the insignia of Chevalier in the Ordre de la Légion d'honneur through the post. No fanfare, just a package and a letter. Although I could not celebrate at the time, Colonel Patrick Bryant, Air and Space Attaché at the French Embassy in the UK, presented me with the award at a ceremony at the Edgbaston Hotel and Conference Centre at Birmingham University on 3 July 2021.

EPILOGUE

For many of those who served, it was not easy to speak out about BP at first, nor was it comfortable to resurface long-forgotten memories. Some of us did not get that chance, while others did not want to break their oath of secrecy. When they signed their name, it was for life.

I mourn that I never had the chance to tell my parents of my work at Bletchley Park and the Pentagon. I would have liked to see pride on their faces for all that I achieved during the war. While I cannot tell them, I can use my time to educate the next generation and those who are new to the story of Bletchley Park.

It took a few attempts, but I finally met Her Majesty Queen Elizabeth. There were a few false starts including a Territorial Army training camp and several Buckingham Palace garden parties, where she was too far away to see more than a glimpse of her in the distance. I was a little closer at an event at the Guildhall in Worcester, but when we lined up to greet Queen Elizabeth and Prince Philip, Her Majesty walked down the row of people lined up against the opposite wall.

I thought I had my chance to meet Her Majesty Queen Elizabeth when a notice appeared in the *London Gazette* on 13 June 2015 to announce my MBE 'for services to remembering and promoting the work of Bletchley Park'. In November I attended the investiture at Buckingham Palace with members of my family and friend, Jill only to discover the Queen was travelling to Birmingham. The occasion was very special, nonetheless. We arrived at Buckingham Palace and were greeted by a member of the Lord Chamberlain's office for a briefing then taken from the Picture Gallery, through the East Gallery into the Ballroom where the investiture was to take place. His Majesty King Charles, as Prince Charles, entered the room and received each person in turn. He was gracious and interested in my connection to Bletchley Park while presenting my insignia. It was over far too quickly, and as I stepped back and marched down the red carpet, I wondered what eighteen-year-old Betty learning her army drills would say if she knew she would one day march in Buckingham Palace!

Finally, in 2021 at an event arranged by the WRAC in the Army and Navy Club in London, I was introduced to Queen Elizabeth and she was as charming and regal as I imagined.

Her Majesty Queen Elizabeth enjoyed a long reign, but I was also around during the reign of her father, George VI between 1936 and 1952, and the short reign in 1936 of his brother Edward VIII. Their father, George V, was on the throne when I was born on 13 May 1923. The list of prime ministers I have seen come and go is even longer; there have been twenty-one up to the point I am writing this, making it five monarchs, twenty-one prime ministers.

So what would my life have been like if there had been no war and no Bletchley Park? I would probably be an old spinster sitting on the porch of Ryecroft, feeding the goats. I would still be playing music and complaining about the transmitter masts in Woofferton ruining my view. My life may have differed in some ways had I not gone to Bletchley, but I would have found a life I was content with. I would still have kept busy with my many interests. Where I am sure my life would have been unimaginably different is in the last two decades – my Bletchley years, part 2.

Giving talks and writing a book have filled these latter years with lots of fun and adventure. I have spoken to interviewers in America, Japan, New Zealand, Canada, France and many in this country. It has been an extraordinary adventure and I am honoured to spend my one-hundredth birthday with friends and family at a party at my Bletchley Park home in the Mansion.

APPENDIX 1

HISTORY OF THE GERMAN POLICE SECTION, 1939–1945

1. From the beginning to the Fall of France

The German Police Section came into being in the Autumn of 1939 when the first substantial break into the system was achieved by Brigadier Tiltman.

This traffic, which was plentiful – 80–100 messages a day – had already been under examination by the French and the Poles, and the latter had made some progress in its cryptographic solution. Sets were allocated at Denmark Hill and Harpenden and a small party of just over a dozen was brought together in Hut 5 for its exploitation.

The system, straightforward double transposition, was used too carelessly to stand up to a concerted effort. Depths were frequent – particularly of messages 180 letters long, the maximum number allowed – and standard beginnings the rule rather than the exception. Above all, the placing of the address at the beginning of the message and the signature at the end made the cryptographer's life a happy one, for addresses in those days were written in full and could run into two full keys length – ANXDE NXBEF EHLSH ABERX DERXO RDNUN GSPOL IZEIX INXFR ANKFU RTXAM XMAIN X. By 1945, this had become XXBDO XFFMX in the middle of the text.

Results, therefore, were quick in coming and decodes began to circulate. Content showed that this source was not likely to provide information of tactical value for our forces in the field, but promised to give a useful picture of what was going on inside Germany and to make it possible to assess the likelihood of internal German collapse. This promise was largely fulfilled. A great deal of information, as to conditions inside Germany accrued and if the indications of internal disintegration were disappointingly few, this was in itself a valuable check to the waves of wishful thinking about the power of the Nazi party, which swept the press and public opinion from time to time throughout the war.

Continued success depended on keeping up the volume and improving the quality of the traffic. The position of Denmark Hill gave that station advantages for a number of wave-lengths, but already in 1939 it was becoming clear that the German Police Network was so widespread and the frequencies it used so various that satisfactory interception could only be achieved by interception spread over a number of different stations at widely different points in the British Isles.

This was not possible until much later, when other successes had given "Y" an important place in the war effort and made available its sets in large numbers. But one advantage we did have then which was lost later and could never be replaced – sets in France.

Located in Metz, these sets were in an ideal position for taking the low frequency traffic that passed in great quantity between the great cities of the Rhine, Ruhr and Westphalian areas. For all their efforts, Denmark Hill (and later Sandridge and Harpenden) could not hold their own with their better-placed French colleagues and it soon became clear that some kind of union of the French and the English effort both in interception and cryptography was desirable. After a good deal of discussion, in which the difficulties of sharing "Y" tasks with the Allies were early in evidence, it was agreed that a mission from England should settle near the French party who were exploiting the traffic under the wing of the Deuxieme Bureau, with its Headquarters at La Férte-Sous-Jouarre. Accordingly in December Lieutenant Colonel Pritchard (then Major) and Lieutenant Colonel Gore-Brown (then Captain) set out with clerks and took up residence at a chateau in this village. The mission was known as "Mission Richard". It had an uphill task, for the French, with individual exceptions, regarded the Mission with the eye of rivalry rather than of friendly co-operation. However the work went on successfully enough to warrant the enlargement of the Mission to a size which would make possible the complete exploitation and production of the decodes from this centre. In February 1940, therefore, a party of 1 officer and 12 men joined Major Pritchard, and all that now remained in England was a traffic section whose job it was to despatch the English-intercepted traffic daily by bag. It was agreed with the French that they should do the even days of the month, we the odd, and this worked quite satisfactorily. It was fairly rare that day failed to break (save Sundays) and the entente, which grew continually more cordially, was never jeopardised by one side breaking a day over which the other had failed. It is worth noting that the French in principal of security allowed only officers to do the work – even the entirely routine work of decoding and typing – and looked askance at the use by us of the other ranks in these tasks. In general, the French showed a prodigality in their expense of manpower (22 officers to our 3 officers and 14 other ranks) and time (lunch at their mess was a matter of three hours with little likelihood of much exacting intellectual effort being possible thereafter).

In early spring Major Pritchard was recalled to England and Captain Dryden took his place. The events of May ascended upon the Mission with only one hint of warning from our source – the urgent summons to prevent a high official from crossing into Holland on the evening of the 9th May. We were first aware of something untoward by the dramatic appearance of Captain Tozer in travel-stained mackintosh and a whirl of cold night wind late on the 10th.

From that time forward interception and with it cryptography began to falter and eventually to cease. It was not to recommence for another three months, when the party, after a sad farewell from the French at Ussel (in the Massif Central, whither French GHQ had drifted), and a successful journey via Bordeaux back to this country, was reconstituted at BP and began once more to take up the threads of the work.

2. August 1940–September 1941

During the period in which the work had been allowed to lapse the Germans had fortunately made no major changes of cypher or network, so that there was little difficulty in getting production going again. Traffic had meanwhile increased, the German Police having spread its net over Western Europe; and an increase in the number of sets to cover it was necessary. This was met by an allocation of 12–16 sets at Beaumanor which quickly became the leading "Domino" (German Police) interception station. It was found useful to detach a member of the traffic section to work at the station, interpreting the needs of the cryptographers to the set room supervisors. Throughout the work of the German Police Section, a special point was made of close liaison with the intercept stations and the value of this became more and more apparent as German Signal and Cypher security became more and more strict.

It was during this period that the first signs of anxiety on the part of the Germans about the security of the cypher was [sic] shown. The German monitoring station in Berlin – always efficient in jumping on minor breaches of discipline – called for a wider variety in the lengths of messages, and this meant an end to the great depths (sometimes up to ten!) of messages 180 letters long. As an added security measure addresses and signatures were placed in the body of the text. Neither of these measures however seriously impeded cryptography for continuity breaking had made available a wide knowledge of the habits of each individual station as well as of the kind of content and jargon to be expected from given texts. There were also from time to time standard cribs (such as the daily report on the rise and fall of the Elbe). But these latter came and went, spotted sooner or later as a source of danger by the Berlin monitors; and it was not so much on these cribs, as on a general "feel" for likely content that the experienced cryptographer came to rely. At an early date all evidence of station idiosyncrasies and forms of address were carded, which facilitated the training of new cryptographers.

With the extension of police activities in Russia the quantity of traffic steadily increased. But here again security measures followed quickly: a separate key and new frequencies were instituted for the Russian traffic.

In quantity this was too small to allow more than 50% success. And the task of breaking the Russian traffic was made harder still when, in August 1941, two sets of keys for each day were introduced in the East. The percentage of breaks for Russian keys was down to 25%, for the "Reich" key 70%. This was the lowest level of success that the section was to show until September of 1944 and the introduction of the "Raster" key. Even so, a fairly steady flow of decodes was available, varying from 30 to 100 a day. The number of staff required to deal with the task had risen to 40.

3. September 1941–November 1942
On September 13th 1941 General Daluege, Chief of the Ordnungs police, sent the following message to the Higher SS and Police Leaders of the forces in Russia:

'The danger of decipherment by the enemy of wireless messages is great. For this reason only such matters are to be transmitted by wireless as can be considered open... Confidential or Secret, but not information which is containing State secrets, calls for especially secret treatment. Into this category fall exact figures of executions (these are to be sent by Courier).'

The General's anxiety about the secrecy of the execution figures is not surprising, for their size was a clear indication of the utter ruthlessness of the Germans in Russia. The anxiety may have been increased by a speech by the Prime Minister drawing the attention of the world to this carnage. In any case, the German security authorities evidently demanded more drastic steps still, and these culminated in a complete change of cypher in mid-September. Double Transposition was dropped (never to appear again) and Double Playfair took its place.

The result was exactly the reverse of what the Germans intended, for whereas the retention of Double Transposition with a still further splitting up of keys would have soon put us out of business, Double Playfair quickly proved to be a most breakable cypher and it became the exception to fail to break a day.

This was the point at which the most considerate increase of staff was required, for there was no reason now why three keys should not be broken daily and three sets of decodes issued. The training school at Bedford was able over a period of 2 or 3 months to meet the need of the cryptographers, but the need for clerks in the traffic sorting and decoding department was harder to fill since the numbers required were larger and the claims of other sections in BP equally great or greater. This is perhaps one of the most important and surprising lessons learnt in the development of a highly specialised organisation such as BP – that it is much easier to get together the skilled part of the train than the unskilled.

In interception, the section was treated with considerable generosity (though never of course satisfied) and the addition of sets at Kedleston Hall (end of 1942) made it possible to keep up with the continual expansion of traffic as the German police force extended its hold over Europe and Russia.

Throughout the Winter of 1942 the Police forces in the East were involved in desperate defensive fighting against the Russian Armies. GP traffic was one of the few sources providing information from this front and it was decided to enlarge the scope of the Intelligence sub-section, under Captain Webster (later Lieutenant Colonel), to give a fuller service of information both externally to the departments receiving the decodes and internally to assist the cryptographers.

In the Spring of 1942 word came from Lieutenant Colonel Crankshaw in Moscow of the Russians' interest in German Police Traffic and our success in exploiting it. A policy of full cooperation was agreed upon from this end, and particulars of the WT network, contents of decodes, and daily keys were sent off. In return, we were to receive traffic from them. This arrived in due course and showed a high standard of interception. As was to be expected, they heard a good deal more of the Eastern traffic, and this was a useful help into breaking the Russian keys. Unfortunately, liaison with the Russians broke down in December, and no more traffic was received. Nor was it ever known what success, if any, the Russians had obtained cryptographically on the material. Some questions put by the Russians to Lieutenant Colonel Crankshaw on our cryptographic technique were of a very elementary kind, but this may have been some obscure kind of bluff.

The cessation of the Russian traffic came at a particularly unfortunate time, for by November the Germans had begun to grow uneasy about the security of straightforward Double-Playfair and introduced their next major cypher alteration.

4. November 1942–August 1944
This change consisted in breaking up the day into 2 hour (subsequently 3 hour) periods, the keys for which were given by permutations of 6 Playfair squares. Thus if the Playfair squares are designated by the letters A to F, the

arrangement might be 0000–0300 hours a key: A + E; 0300–0600: E + C; 0600–0900 D + A and so on.

This was obviously a considerable advance in security for it reduced the amount of traffic on any one key from about 100 messages to (at most) 20. But it had its own weaknesses: thus traffic was always heaviest in the middle of the day and it was soon possible to get the two midday groups out. This would often provide 4 out of the 6 Playfair squares for the day and other groups would turn out to be further permutations of these four. A technique was soon devised for deriving an unknown square when one square was known. There was also carelessness by the Germans in the permutations used, so that square A + B might be used for one period, and square B + A for another. This at once revealed itself in the bigram count, and made breaking much easier.

After some rough going, therefore, the section came out into smoother waters and by February 1943 was producing between 4 and 500 decodes a week.

Besides change of the cypher the Germans had always three other security measures at their disposal: change of the call-signs; change of the network; and break-up of geographical area covered by any one key.

The first of these was frequently resorted to – on an average there seemed to be a complete change of call-signs every six months. This never worried us very much, as continuity in breaking made it possible quickly to break new groups and extract the call-sign information from the addresses and signature in the text. Moreover German wireless disclipline was never quite equal to a complete change of this sort, and the CRR staffs at the Y-stations had a great time with indiscretions and howlers that appeared in the logs, and competed in friendly rivalry with each other and with "Source" for the production of the first full list.

Network changes were also frequent. But here again continuity of work in the log-sections both at BP and the Y-stations reduced the disturbance caused thereby to a minimum. The tendency on the part of the Germans was to employ more and more frequencies, and the chief problem that this set was that of adequate coverage.

The third security measure taken by the Germans – the splitting up of the geographical area covered by one key – was more troublesome. It meant that as soon as a block of traffic was detached from the main key and given a key of its own – as happened gradually for traffic in France, Holland, Norway, Italy, Romania, Poland – it became largely unreadable. This was partly owing to the fact that no individual country produced enough traffic to give breakable groups (when chopped into 3 hourly time periods) and partly owing to lack of staff available to cope with the many borderline groups which might or might not be breakable. Thus, though the results on the main German key were increasingly satisfactory throughout 1943, there was always the painful awareness of how much was going unbroken. Some figures will illustrate this. The decodes for October 1943 reached the highest number ever recorded in the history of the section – over 3000. And during two weeks of that month over 70 keys were broken, with almost 100% success for the main German key. At the same time the total of traffic received during these weeks was no fewer than 1760 messages, and was made up as follows:

Solo key for greater Germany 598
Poker key for France 327

Banker key for Italy 313
Rummy key for Croatia 167
Patience key for Poland 141
Pontoon key for Hungary & Norway 58
Bridge key for general practice 131
Nap key for South Russia 4
Whist key for Riga 21

Of these keys it was only the first that could be broken with any certainty and the record of groups broken for this particular week reads: Solo 46; Poker 8; Banker 2; Rummy 1; Nap 2.

This widespread splitting-up of keys was not however wholly unfortunate; for it resulted in very frequent re-encodings from key to key and from one day to the next. In this way an entry could generally be made into the smaller keys when time and staff were available to man it.

The very high traffic totals being achieved by the Autumn of 1944 were in part due to the fact that there was more traffic passing, and in part due to better coverage. By mid-1943 Kedleston Hall was fully operational on Domino, and a few sets were available also at Sandridge. This, with the sets at WOYG, gave a good all-round cover. A switch-over of WOYG sets to Shenley in the Spring of 1944 (WOYG was required for second front cover) only caused a temporary set-back, for the enthusiasm with which Shenley threw themselves into the problems of Domino cover quickly brought their effectiveness up to and even beyond that of Kedleston Hall.

In order to handle this large and complex daily load of traffic and to see as much as possible of it through in decode form to the ministries, a staff of 84 was barely adequate. This was divided into the sub-sections: Traffic – Cryptography – Decoding – Emending and Issuing. The Intelligence Section, though smaller, was no less important, for not only was the content of the decodes of increasing interest, but also the success in getting it depended more and more upon efficient checking for reincodements and other services which were part of the intelligence sub-section's work.

One particularly useful item of this sort was a standard daily report from the Police Flying Squadron in Poland and the Balkans. It began to appear in July of 1944 and seemed to promise an easy life for the cryptographers for the rest of the time. This promise was not of course fulfilled. Very quickly in fact it was succeeded by a most ominous threat: that of a complete change of cypher. The threat became reality on the first of September 1944.

5. September 1944–VE Day
The new cypher – "Raster" was its name – was by far the best hand-cypher which the Germans devised. A daily changing stencil with a good starting-point indicator system, it looked at first sight unbreakable. But from an examination of a captured Army pad one weakness appeared: the daily stencil of 24 lines was made by an arbitrary choice out of a set of 36 master rods (or leads) held by the printers. This at once gave cryptography a chance. The limitations imposed by this feature were catalogued by the Hollerith Section and, with the help of the Police Flying Squadron crib, it was found possible to break the main German key after all. The drawback was the increase in the time-lag between receipt of the traffic and issue of decodes. During the Double-Playfair period

it was always possible (with reasonable good luck) to produce clear text within 24 hours of the transmission of the message. With Raster the time-lag increased to a week or more, for the initial breaks, which at first were the print of cribs of 60–80 letters, only supplied 6–8 lines of the stencil, and the task of extending this patch upward and downward was slow and laborious.

The prospect became still gloomier when, after some 3 weeks, the one short crib which we possessed disappeared. But the difficulties of Raster were not all on our side; the Germans too were making heavy weather of this exacting new cypher. The result was a steady flow of incorrect encodings followed by their correct reincodement. It was from these that the Section now drew its life-blood. They increased rather than diminished and enabled the section to survive yet another improvement in the system which the Germans introduced after two months. This was the addition of other basic sets of 36 rods from which the stencils could be printed. From captured Army pads we were able to analyse all new sets and the number steadily crept up, until 17 different ones were identified, recorded and catalogued. Theoretically this meant that we had 17 times the work now to do for every solution that we had when faced with the single original set. But by this time (Spring 1945) German cypher discipline was swiftly declining, and the number of false encodements, resendings and howlers of every sort was very considerable. But for this, it can be said that the Raster cypher had now reached a point at which further exploitation would have been uneconomical – without the enlistment of high-grade machinery.

Some work was indeed done in this direction, and though it was clear that the machinery necessary for a cryptographic attack would have to be of the most complicated kind, a practical result of the research work done was the construction of a machine for decoding from known stencils.

The content of the messages was, naturally, of increasing interest, and provides as a whole a singular picture of the last days of the Nazi regime and of its individual leaders. For this reason cryptographic work was continued long after VE Day (no police-keys were ever captured) and the final results in the battle against this formidable cypher were very satisfactory, the best months being February and March 1945 when only 6 and 3 days respectively were missed.

The work of breaking Raster was the most exacting kind of cryptography – interminable searching through catalogues of figures for the correct position out of many thousands, which, if missed by a moment of inattention, meant the failure of the day. It is appropriate therefore at this point to pay a work of tribute to the ream of cryptographers who stuck at the problem with such determination.

Conclusion

The contribution of the German Police Section to the war effort was not of the sensational kind. Its task, when the lights went out in Europe, was that of peering unremittingly into the gloom, and of lifting a corner of the blackout here and there. But the results, even if not of the kind that make headlines, and history, were certainly such as Intelligence staffs came ultimately to value almost as much: the kind of information that, piece by piece, builds up a background of knowledge upon which decisions can be based.

The cost, in terms of men and material, was very considerable. If the personnel of the Y-stations devoted exclusively or almost exclusively to German Police are included, the total number of people involved in the task at its widest expansion would be not far short of 500. It was worked out at one time (by a purist whose place was clearly in the Treasury) that the cost to the Country was about £4 per decode. When the decode happens to be a request by an NCO of police in the Ukraine for an extra issue of underpants, the question naturally suggests itself: was it worth it?

The answer depends on whether one thinks that the war – and "Y" – could have been waged in any but a total way. In any war effort there are clearly things which are more rewarding and others which are less so, but the essence of Britain's effort in this war was its totality; and, in this, "Y" shared. There are good grounds for arguing that "Y" must be considered totally or not at all. To neglect one part is to deprive the effort as a whole of data – cryptographic and otherwise – which may have a part to play later and in other contexts. To abandon any part altogether is to run the risk of being unable to pick up the threads again.

The story of the German Police Section illustrates well both the interdependence of the various elements in "Y", and the supreme importance of continuity. Experience in the breaking of the Police cyphers made possible an entry first into German Air Medium Grade. Both these sections were at first off-shoots of the Police Section, and their cryptographers trained by a kind of graduation through police material. The value of continuity is sufficiently clearly illustrated by the final success of "Raster". It is safe to say that without the great fund of knowledge and experience accumulated through months of continuous breaking, the attack on Raster would have ended in failure.

It is unlikely that the exact cryptographic problems set by German Police Traffic will ever present themselves again; the knowledge of their solution was shared not only by our allies the Americans, Russians, French and Poles, but also by the Germans themselves – but the grounding in general cryptographic technique to be gained from a study of them may service future generations of cryptographers well.

As to the story that the German Police Decodes tell, it is not, as observed already, of the sensational kind; but it should help future generations to appreciate (if they are one day to be allowed to profit by the labours of these years) the efficiency and ruthlessness of the machine which so nearly overwhelmed Britain in World War.

APPENDIX 2

BRITISH LEGION POLICE FORCE REPORT 1938

Below is my father's report on the abandoned British
Legion Police Force mission to Czechoslovakia:

BRITISH LEGION AGM
LUDLOW
21 October 1938

*As a very ordinary member of the British Legion, it is a great
honour to have to give an account of the all too brief life of
the Volunteer Police Force, which was created almost at a
moment's notice for service in Czechoslovakia. It may be called
an offspring of the Legion and though it died so young, it was
indeed a very sturdy child – as the events from October 5th to
15th go to prove.*

*To go back a few weeks to about the middle of September –
the F.O. asked our National Chairman if he could raise a force of
10,000 legionnaires should they be required. You have no doubt
about his reply.*

*Later, political circumstances changed the whole situation
and Sir Francis Fetherston-Godley was asked again by the F.O.
if he could create a body of 1,200 Volunteer Police from the
Legion for service at once in the Plebiscite area.*

*On Wednesday Oct 5th all branches received memos calling
for volunteers. As time was pressing, the onus was put on the*

County Secretaries, who were to have the application forms before 6 o/c that evening.

The result was that in two days, 17,000 applications had been received and the Force of 1,200 complete and equipped was ready to sail on Friday night. Three days after the memos were sent out from H.Q.

On arrival at Olympia, each man received his identity card and then filed into his contingency site, one of the two galleries round the Empire Hall. After being well satisfied by Messrs J. Lyons & Co, each man filled a canvas Palliasse and pillow with straw and drew 2 blankets (or more). After which it was not long before every man had received his blue suit and badge, belt, stick, gloves and Legion tie, haversack, water bottle, 2 shirts, 2 towels and cleaning materials. Metropolitan police great coats and caps, the next morning, completed the issue.

The Force had its own fleet of Bedford Motor Vans and motorcycles for despatch riders and a St Johns Ambulance unit.

On the Saturday morning, the whole Force marched out with the Band of the Welsh Guards. The Legion standard bearer alongside the Guards Colours made a fine show. The O.C. addressed the Force in Empire Hall after the parade and expressed his appreciation of the performance. Twenty years after demobilization (from the First World War 1918) and every man marching with a swing. He added the main point of the march was to see if the boots pinched!

Sir Philip Morris also gave the Force a cheery address and told how he had flown over to see Herr Hitler who cordially welcomed the scheme and said when the BLVPF [British Legion Volunteer Police Force] *was used in the Plebiscite areas, German troops would <u>not</u> be employed. On this occasion too, General Sir Ian Hamilton mounted a trestle table and gave his welcome and was greeted with the most tremendous cheers.*

Lady Spencer Churchill, who had taken charge of the comforts of the men, had a great reception when she announced that she had rung up Imperial Tobacco Co and asked for 60,000 cigarettes 'on tick'. The reply was 'no tick, you can have them'.

Following a senior officer's visit to the Foreign Office the Plebiscite would not take place and consequently the operation was cancelled.

I have no further information, but it is a hope that someone reading this book will be able to let me know more about the exercise.

GLOSSARY

ATS – Auxiliary Territorial Service (the women's army).

BAS – British Army Staff.

Block F – One of the largest blocks at Bletchley Park, which was first occupied in November 1943.

Bombe – Electro–mechanical machine, designed by Alan Turing and Gordon Welchman, used to find the settings and wheel orders of the Enigma machine by testing a guessed phrase or word (crib).

Call sign – A group of letters or numbers sent to identify the sender or recipient.

Cipher/Cypher – One letter, number or symbol of plain language substituted for another for the purpose of making it unintelligible without the means to reverse it.

Code – A word, phrase or figure substituted by another to change, abbreviate or alter its meaning and can be reversed (decoded) with the aid of a codebook.

Depths – Several messages of the same length enciphered using the same key.

Domino – Codename for German Police Section ciphers.

Double Playfair – A cipher system enciphering a message using 25 letters of the alphabet laid out in a 5 x 5 square, then enciphering the result on another square.

Double Transposition – A cipher system whereby the plain language letters of an enciphered version of a message are rearranged according to the specific setting, then enciphered again on the same or different settings.

Enigma – German machine with a keyboard, rotors and in some machines a plugboard used to encipher and decipher messages using a complex electrical process.

GC&CS – Government Code and Cypher School.

GCHQ – Government Communications Headquarters, formerly known as GC&CS.

Hand cypher/cipher – A cipher where a message is enciphered by hand without machinery.

Hut 3 – The section for translating and processing the traffic deciphered in Hut 6. The sections in Huts 3, 4, 6 and 8 retained the name of the hut even after moving to another building.

Hut 4 – The hut dealing with enemy naval ciphers; translating and processing the German naval traffic deciphered in Hut 8.

Hut 5 – The hut housing some of Military Section until moving to Block F in 1943.

Hut 6 – The section breaking the Enigma messages of the German army and air force.

Intercept – A signal obtained by interception; the act of listening to and recording messages sent by wireless telegraphy (W/T).

Key – The settings for enciphering or deciphering text; a specific Enigma cipher such as Orange.

NAAFI – Navy, Army, Air Force Institutes providing catering facilities such as canteens, shops etc.

Paraphrase – To change the phrasing of a message but not its meaning.

PNEU – Parents National Educational Union.

RAF – Royal Air Force.

Raster – A hand cipher system as a substitute for Double Playfair using a stencil to encipher/decipher a message and the position of the transposition determined by the underlying blocked out squares beneath.

Roulette – Enigma key used by senior German police officials.

SIS – Secret Intelligence Service (MI6).

SIXTA – Section responsible for the Traffic Analysis of German networks other than naval.

Stencil – A piece of paper or cardboard with holes through which messages are written onto paper beneath to encipher and decipher a message.

TA – Territorial Army; in codebreaking it means Traffic Analysis – the study of intercepts to gather intelligence.

TGD – Enigma key used by the German Security Police.

Traffic – Messages in any form passed or prepared for transmission by electronic means.

WAAF – Women's Auxiliary Air Force.

WRAC – Women's Royal Army Corps (replaced the ATS on 1 February 1949).

WRNS – Women's Royal Naval Service, often referred to as Wrens.

W/T – Wireless telegraphy.

Y Station – A station set up to intercept enemy messages sent by W/T.

4IS – No. 4 Intelligence School, Military Section.

6IS – No. 6 Intelligence School, Military Section. Became SIXTA in 1944.

A copy of the 1944 Cryptographic Dictionary held in The National Archives (HW25/33) can be viewed online at https://www.codesandciphers.org.uk/documents/cryptdict/cryptix.htm.

BIBLIOGRAPHY

Bourne, S. *Under Fire: Black Britain in Wartime 1939–45.* The History Press. 2021.

Copeland, J. (ed). *Colossus, The Secrets of Bletchley Park's Codebreaking Computers, (Chapter 17: Codebreaking and Colossus by Donald Mitchie).* Oxford University Press. 2006.

Dunlop, T. *Army Girls: The secrets and stories of military service from the final few women who fought in World War II.* Headline. 2021.

Gallehawk, J., Howard, K. (eds). *Figuring it out at Bletchley Park: 1939–1945.* Redditch. 2007.

Hinsley, F.H., Stripp, A. *Codebreakers: The Inside Story of Bletchley Park.* Oxford University Press. 2001.

Hinsley, F.H., Thomas, E.E., Ransom, C.F.G. and Knight, R.C. *British Intelligence in the Second World War. The German Police Section.* Vol. 2. H.M. Stationery Office. 1981.

Hinsley, F.H., *British Intelligence in the Second World War, Abridged Edition.* H.M. Stationery Office. 1993.

Liberty, H. *The Forgotten Giant of Bletchley Park: Brigadier John Tiltman.* Pen and Sword Military. 2022.

Roberts, J., O'Connell, P. *Lorenz: Breaking Hitler's Top Secret Code at Bletchley Park.* The History Press. 2017.

Smith, M. *The Debs of Bletchley Park and other stories.* Aurum Press. 2015.

Smith, M. *The Secrets of Station X: How the Bletchley Park Codebreakers Helped Win the War*. Biteback Publishing. 2011.

Thirsk, J. *Bletchley Park: An Inmate's Story*. ISO-Galago. 2008.

Turing, D. *The Codebreakers of Bletchley Park: The Secret Intelligence Station that Helped Defeat the Nazis*. Arcturus Publishing Ltd. 2020.

Watkins, G. *Cracking the Luftwaffe Codes: The Secrets of Bletchley Park*. Frontline. 2013.

Papers from the National Archives

A History of British Sigint 1914–42 Vol 1, Frank Birch HW43/1

A History of British Sigint 1942–45 Vol 2, Frank Birch HW 43/2

Commander Bradshaw General Orders, HW14/144

History of the German Police Section, TNA HW3/155

History of Military Intelligence, HW3/92

Letter to Winston Churchill dated 21 October 1941 requesting more staff and 'Action this day' response, HW1/155

Memorandum by Mr de Grey dated 17 August 1949, TNA HW50/50

MI5 Report on Wynn Angell and Georges Dobrynine, TNA HS9/437/5

Security Breaches 1943–45, HW62/8

Staff List of 4IS dated 2 December 1940, HW14/9

Staff List of 4IS dated 13 July 1942, HW14/143

Original letters

Letters from Walter Penrose Sharp to Betty Webb, 2003–2010, author's own copy

Letter from John Burrows to Betty Webb, 1995, author's own copy

Letter from Margaret Rock to Alice Rock, 1940, courtesy of Charles and Jane Foster

Articles/Reports

Center for Cryptographic History, National Security Agency 2007, Brigadier John Tiltman: A Giant Among Cryptanalysts https:media.defense.gov/2021/Jul/13/20002761958/-1/-1/TILTMAN.PDF

Morrison, Kathryn, English Heritage 'A Maudlin and Monstrous Pile': The Mansion at Bletchley Park, Buckinghamshire

Cheetham, T., Bletchley Park Trust, 'The Camps' RAF Church Green and Shenley Road Military Camp

Lydekker, J, unpublished memoir, courtesy of Liz Lydekker

Online Sources

Regulations for the Auxiliary Territorial Services 1941, accessed at https://nla.gov.au/nla.obj-203848952/view?partId=nla.obj-203866237

West India Service Committee Circulars accessed at https://westindiacommittee.org

John Herivel's letter of thanks to Newmanry staff dated 10 July 1945 accessed at https://artsandculture.google.com/asset/letter-to-of-thanks-to-staff-from-john-herivel-head-of-the-newmanry/WwEDTObb-o7s_Q?hl=en

Other

Charlotte Vine-Stevens/Betty Webb Service Record from the Ministry of Defence – used for references to service and quotes from service record forms

Motor Transport Corps Logbook, Bletchley Park Trust